"ETIQUETTE — *that's just fluff!*"

Hank exclaimed when his sister, Sylvia, chided him for not holding open the front door for her. "If you ask me, I'll take brains and ability — and skip the manners — to show what a person's worth."

Whoa there, Hank! The person who has brains and ability *without* good manners may never get a chance to prove his worth. His poor manners will antagonize others — both in business and social activities.

You know how *you* feel when you're walking or driving along the street and someone cuts sharply in front of you. He may be someone you know or a total stranger, but you certainly don't feel friendly towards him.

On the other hand, there's the boy who stops to help you when you have a flat. He's a stranger, but you feel as if you'd like to have him for a friend — almost as if he were a friend.

In short, the Golden Rule is still the best of all rules. And that's just what etiquette is. It's a way of showing that you're friendly and thoughtful of the other fellow, that you appreciate his thoughtfulness of you.

Try it and you'll see. — Gay Head

To my mother —
the most thoughtful
the most courteous
person I've ever known

Sincere thanks to
Nancy Scandrett
and
Mary Dirlam
for their invaluable assistance
in the preparation of certain chapters

CONTENTS

WHAT YOU SAY
. . . when making introductions

WOULD you rather take six aptitude tests than make one introduction? Would you rather face a firing line than a receiving line?

Then cheer up—and settle down to learning the *whys* and *wherefores* of introductions. There aren't many; they aren't difficult. They simplify, rather than complicate, this business of introducing people. And, once you have these simple formulas fixed in your mind, you won't worry about making a fumble.

First, introduce men and boys *to* women and girls; and younger people *to* older people. In translation, this means to mention first the name of the person *to whom* you're making the introduction. (When the introduction involves two people of the same sex and approximately the same age, the order doesn't matter.)

Right: Mother, this is Chad Bowles.

Wrong: Chad, I'd like you to meet my mother.

Right: Mr. Walser, this is my kid brother, Bill.

Wrong: Bill, meet Mr. Walser, principal of Jefferson High.

Next, make your introduction as simple and uncluttered as possible. Introduce one person to another, instead of doubling up and introducing both people to each other.

The Hard Way: Betty, this is Ed Stokes. Ed, this is Betty Copeland.

The Easy Way: Betty Copeland, this is Ed Stokes.

QUESTION MARKS

When to use Mr. or Miss, instead of first names?

Only when you would usually address the person that way. Your own friends are presented as Paul O'Malley, Jean Dart, and Sam Steiner. Your teacher and your next-door neighbor would naturally be Miss Jamison and Mr. Arnold. The exceptions are relatives whose last names differ from yours, such as your stepfather and your married sister. Introduce them as "My father (or stepfather), Mr. Reed," and "My sister, Mrs. Talmadge."

How do you introduce people with titles, such as doctors and clergymen?

A doctor, a dentist, a minister with a doctor of divinity degree, or an educator with a doctor's degree should be introduced as "Doctor"; a bishop as "Bishop"; a rabbi as "Rabbi"; a priest as "Father"; other clergymen as "Mister"; a member of a sisterhood as "Sister"; a judge as "Judge"; and a mayor as "His Honor, Mayor ———."

Which introductory phrases are "acceptable"?

Any of these:

"Mrs. Peacock, I'd like to introduce my cousin, Cathy Brewster."

"Shirley Dawes, I'd like you to meet Harry Payne."

"Phyllis Devine, this is my cousin, Bob O'Ruark."

"Tom Bost, Arthur Fetzer."

But it's taboo to give orders—"Shirley, meet Harry Payne" or "Tom, shake hands with Arthur." And "May I present . . . ?" is more formal than most of the introductions you'll make.

Suppose you forget someone's name? Don't cover up by mumbling, "This is James Blurp." Come right out with, "I'm sorry, James, I don't remember your last name." James will answer your S.O.S., never fear.

How to acknowledge an introduction?

You're always safe with "How do you do," and you're more likely to make a hit if you add the other person's name to your greeting. "Hello" is all right if only young people are present. It shows more respect for older people to say, "How do you do."

Frills, such as "Charmed, I'm sure" or "Pleased to meet you," sound insincere. If you've looked forward to meeting Polly Franklin, say so with a straightforward, "I'm very glad to know you, Polly." But don't embarrass her by adding a vague "Oh, I've heard *so much* about you!" If you really have heard complimentary remarks about her, tell the source. "My cousin, Tom Bobbitt, says you're his favorite dance partner!"

When do you shake hands?

Handshaking is always in order when men and boys are introduced to each other. The matter is optional when a boy is introduced to a girl—and it's the girl's option! But if the boy unwittingly makes the first move, the girl should meet him halfway, instead of leaving him with his hand dangling in mid-air. And do make yours a firm, brief handclasp, not one of the prolonged-pumping or flabby-fisted varieties.

Must you always stand up for introductions?

The ups-and downs of introductions are easy when you follow these two general rules: (1) A boy always rises to the occasion, no matter whom he's meeting or greeting. (2) It's a "must" for a girl to stand only on being introduced to older people, although it would be courteous of her to rise to greet another girl who's already standing.

What about the confusion of double introductions?

That's an easy one—there's no confusion! Here's what happens when two couples meet and only the boys know each other:

DAVE *(to his date)*: Sue Michaels, this is Hank Gibson.

SUE: How do you do, Hank.

HANK: How do you do. *(Turning to his date)* Rosemary Clark, I'd like you to meet Sue Michaels and Dave Burke.

ROSEMARY: How do you do.

SUE AND DAVE: How do you do, Rosemary.

FILLING THE GAP

Your responsibility doesn't end with introductions. It's up to you to fill the awkward pause that may follow the how-do-you-do's. Don't direct your remarks to one person. Swing the conversation into some channel where all of you can navigate equally well.

Bring the third person up to date on the conversation: "Stuart and I were arguing about 'hot rods' as a highway menace. What's your opinion, Ralph?" or "We've been trying to decide which movie to see. Have you any suggestions, Mrs. Entwistle?"

Extend an invitation to the person who has just joined you: "Doris and I are on our way to the library, Helen. Would you like to come along?" or "Won't you join us for a soda, Harold?"

Or, as a last resort, identify one friend for the other: "Sally was my bunkmate at camp last summer, Enid." But don't make your identification tags too personal, such as "Connie is going steady with 'Tarzan' Oaks, so beware!" or, "All the girls think Baxter is the best looking boy in school!"

A good host, no matter how busy, always starts the conversation *before* he abandons newly-met guests. But if your host neglects this, the first conversational attempt is up to the person to whom the introduction was made.

What can you say to someone you've just met?

A thousand things, from airplanes to zoos, and including radio, TV, books, movies, records, and sports.

"Have you ever flown? I'm trying to talk my folks into letting me take a plane when I visit my aunt in San Francisco next month."

"Have you read *The Conquest of Everest?* I'm making a book report on it next week."

"Did you get to see any of the World Series? I was lucky enough to watch a telecast of the last game."

MEET THE FOLKS

Don't save your welcome mat for large, pre-arranged parties. You're automatically labeled "host" or "hostess" when you have even *one* guest in your home.

If the family circle is in the living room when your date arrives, make a general introduction: "Folks, this is Jack Saunders. Jack, I'd like you to meet my mother, my father, my uncle—Mr. Pinero—and my brother, George." You'd introduce a girl the same way.

(At school your teachers are host and hostesses. Introduce your mother to Miss Stark—even though Miss Stark is the younger of the two—but in the case of Mr. Gaines, the rule of introducing men *to* women holds: "Mother, this is Mr. Gaines, my science teacher.")

PARTY LINE

As a party hostess, you should see that all your guests meet each other. But that doesn't call for a round robin of introductions for every new arrival. Your introductions will be useless if you pop them off in rapid-fire succession. Present the newcomer to a small group of people, at first—"Jane Parker, I'd like you to meet Phyllis Croft, Mark Arbisi, and Dan Walsek. Jane and I went hosteling together last summer." Later in the evening, catch up with Jane and introduce her to anyone she hasn't met.

What to do if so many guests arrive at once that you can't do the honors all around? Just announce: "I'm going to leave you 'on your own' and ask you to introduce yourselves." Later, you can check to see that any two who might be particularly congenial have met. Or you can rescue any unusually shy guests who don't seem to be mixing with the others.

PRESENTING — YOU!

You needn't wait for introductions when you're a guest at a private party. Meet your fellow guests halfway by offering, "We haven't met, have we? I'm Ted Hughes."

The girl to whom you speak will reply, "How do you do. I'm Beth Crosby," and you take it from there as if you'd been introduced by your hostess. Or, if it's a dating affair, the boys first introduce themselves to each other, then their dates.

The same technique holds good for introducing yourself to receiving lines. But tone it down to a restrained "Good evening. I'm Robert Collins." Very often, the first person in the line will repeat your name to the next person,—"Mr. Hammer, I'd like to introduce Robert Collins." Your reply of course, is "How do you do, Mr. Hammer"—and so on down the line.

The chaperons at a party or dance, too, deserve at least a moment of your attention. Take time to introduce yourself to them and make some comment, such as, "The decorations are most unusual, aren't they?" Then they'll remember you as "that charming Hazel Hopkins" instead of "that tall thin girl who didn't look at us all evening."

At a school affair, be sure to greet the principal and any teachers who are present. Identify yourself by name and grade—Raymond Wetzel, 10-A—so they can place you immediately.

With fellow students, of course, you're more casual. It's friendly, not forward, to say hello to the new girl in your math class. But never neglect introductions. Don't settle for a "Hi, there!" Welcome her with, "Hello, I'm Frank Ward. You're new at Central High, aren't you?"

In business, it's necessary to add some remark to identify yourself. You could start an interview with a prospective employer by saying, "Good morning, Mr. Marino. I'm Dan Skalla. Mr. Knowles suggested that I see you about an opening in your shipping department." And when you're new on a job, you'd explain to the other employees, "I'm Nancy Forkner, Mr. Lamb's new typist."

An explanation would also be necessary if you met an acquaintance who didn't seem to remember you. Help him over his embarrassment with, "I'm Vivian de Camp. We met at Pat Nelson's clam bake last summer."

THE LAST WORD

Good-byes are as important as hellos. What if you didn't have much to say during the brief chat between David and his cousin Jonathan? You were introduced to Jonathan, and it's rude to turn your back on him abruptly when you leave. It's unnecessary, too. There's no tongue-twisting about "I'm glad I met you" or "I've enjoyed meeting you." If you feel more enthusiastic about him, you might say, "I hope to see you again soon."

And if Jonathan beats you to it with some such comment, you're being paid a compliment. A careless "Sure thing" or "Likewise" or "Same here" isn't good enough. Your sincere "Thank you" is what's needed to put a fine finishing touch to an introduction.

WHAT YOU SAY
. . . in conversation

"NICE day, isn't it?"

"Yes, it certainly is."

"Good to see the sun shining."

"Especially after all the rain we've been having."

"Rainy days are depressing, aren't they?"

"Very. And it's been so chilly, too."

Had enough? YES! Then let's do something about it. Not about the weather—about the conversation. Let's find other things to talk about and other ways to keep the conversational ball rolling.

Let's listen to two conversations that Bruce O'Conner had with two girls at a dance:

BRUCE: That's a pretty dress you have on, Ann. I like the color.

ANN: Oh, thanks.

BRUCE *(after pause):* You know, girls are lucky about clothes. They can choose unusual colors. Boys' clothes are always the same—blue, brown, gray.

ANN: Yes, that's true.

BRUCE *(after another pause):* Of course, we can add a dash of color in ties and socks—

ANN: Yes, you can.

(Long silence)

BRUCE: Well, that's the end of the number. Thanks, Ann.

(Bruce leaves Ann with her next partner and joins Beth for the next dance.)

BRUCE: That's a pretty dress you have on, Beth. I like the color.

BETH: Oh, I'm glad you do. It's one of those new shades with the silly names.

BRUCE: What's it called?

BETH: Cinnamon, of all things! What's more, the same dress comes in mustard, sage, and paprika. You'd think you were buying spices at a grocery store, wouldn't you?

BRUCE *(laughing):* No wonder fashion ads are a mystery to us fellows. And here I thought you were just wearing a pretty brown dress. . . .

Now give a guess as to which of these two girls Bruce asked for a date the next Saturday night. You don't need more than one guess, do you? The difference between the two girls had nothing to do with their looks or clothes, either. It was as simple as this: Beth was easy to talk to; Ann wasn't.

Does Beth have a formula for conversational success? Yes, and this is it: Beth gives twice as much thought to the person she's talking with as she does to herself. People who get conversational paralysis aren't necessarily conceited—in fact, they may be overly shy—but they do spend too much time thinking of themselves. Instead of asking themselves how they can put the other person at ease, they're preoccupied with questions like these: What does he (or she) think of me? What kind of impression am I making? How do I look?

HI, STRANGER!

Now let's analyze a "first conversation" between two people who've just met:

RALPH: So you're from Greenville?

SALLY: That's right.

RALPH: A good friend of mine lives there—Jack Ferrabee. Know him?

SALLY: No, I don't.

RALPH: Well, how about Alice Stranahan? Know her?

SALLY: No, I don't think so.

RALPH: Then maybe you know her cousin, Bob Steele?

SALLY: Uh, no, I—

This can be called the "Do you know . . ." routine, which usually develops into a wild-goose chase. Even if Ralph and Sally do "connect" on some innocent victim whom they both know, not much conversation will come of it. Very likely there'll be a polite discussion which may somewhat dissect the victim but which won't tell Ralph and Sally much about each other.

There was nothing wrong with Ralph's opening question, but Sally could have given him a better response: "Yes, and Greenville's a fine town to live in! We have a new Municipal Park with a lake and a dance pavilion. Have you heard about it?" Or: "Yes, it's the town that's been in the news recently. Did you read about our new atomic energy plant?"

Either of these remarks would have given Ralph a good lead. Whether his answer was *yes* or *no,* he could have taken the ball from there and the couple would have been off on a lively discussion instead of a "Do you know . . .?" session that ends in a dull thud.

Even if Sally hadn't gotten into the swing of things right away, Ralph might have tried a gentle needling, such as: "Greenville, uh-hum. Your baseball team doesn't seem to be setting the league on fire this year, does it?" Perhaps Sally isn't a sports fan, but her local pride will be sure to make her come to the defense of the Greenville nine!

Here's another "first conversation" at a very different pace:

DONNA: Are you interested in photography? My brother has been giving me some lessons in camera technique and —

JACK: Is he a camera fan? I'll have to meet him because —

DONNA: Yes, he's received several prizes for —

JACK: Speaking of prizes. I won an exposure meter in a contest that —

DONNA: Oh, an exposure meter! Bud's been saving up to buy one. He —

Whew! Takes your breath away, doesn't it? Donna and Jack are going to be breathless, too, pretty soon. What's more, they're not going to like each other very much, because neither will let the other get more than two words in edgewise.

Donna and Jack were in luck, if they'd only realized it. They'd hit on a topic that interested both of them.

An exchange of information might have been the basis for a solid friendship. But you can't learn anything—or learn about anyone—if you won't let the other fellow have a chance to talk, too.

Jack should have allowed Donna to finish her first sentence before he introduced a new idea. And Donna should have played fair by returning the favor.

A conversation is a cooperative venture, not

a competitive one. You're trying to strike up a friendship and exchange ideas, not "hog" the show.

And here's one more conversation to listen to:

DOTTIE: What a simply terrific game that was last night! I almost died of excitement.

CHET: You ain't kidding! Believe you me, I've never sat through such an exciting quarter as the last one—and that's for sure.

DOTTIE: Central really has a terrific team this year. I'd have died if we hadn't won. I simply would've.

CHET: They sure was out to get us last night, but we shown 'em what for, eh, baby?

DOTTIE: We really did. It was simply terrific.

CHET: You can say that again. I bet that coach still don't know what hit him.

DOTTIE: I'll simply die if we don't get the championship. Won't it be terrific if we do?"

Get the idea? Take the words "die," "simply," and "terrific," away from Dottie's conversation and what's left? Not much. No wonder most of the people who talk to Dottie weary of her — they feel as worn out as the few words she has in her vocabulary.

Chet has the mistaken notion that correct speech is sissy stuff; he thinks his sloppy English demonstrates his "toughness." Actually, however, sloppy English is like a sloppy appearance: it indicates that you have little respect for other people and less for yourself.

Pay attention to speech. Don't overuse slang expressions; build up a wide vocabulary. And use good English every single day. That's the only way to be sure you'll use it on important occasions, such as job interviews or first meetings with people you're eager to impress favorably.

WHAT TO TALK ABOUT

Topics of conversation are as varied as people themselves. But you don't find things to talk about by sitting at home and twiddling your thumbs. You find them by going about alertly, with your eyes and ears and mind open.

You stop, look, and listen, in stores and restaurants, on buses and trolleys, in school and out.

You read magazine articles on sports and science, as well as fashions and movie stars (if you're a girl); articles on personalities in the news and new developments in fabrics and home appliances, as well as sports and science (if you're a boy). You read newspapers and discover that, in addition to the comics section, sports, and society pages, there are editorials, political columns, and letters to the editor.

You listen to the radio and watch TV and realize that comedy and disc jockey programs have competition in the form of good dramatic programs, stimulating discussion programs, news commentators, and interviews.

You go to the library and instead of heading straight for the mystery and adventure sections, you browse around and find there are also books of short stories, plays, and essays, biographies and travel books.

You absorb all of these things — the trivial as well as the important. And then when the conversation bogs down, you lift it up with:

"I read the most exasperating letter in the *News* today. It was from a man who insisted that all teen-agers were reckless drivers."

"Have you been in Bullard's Department Store recently? They're having an exhibit of high school art and there's one water color painting of a picnic that's most amusing."

"I stopped by the Sugar Bowl yesterday and had a new dish called an 'Atomic Bombe.' Guess what was in it!"

"While I was in the library last night, I picked up a book on handwriting. I'm almost tempted to take up handwriting analysis as a hobby. Here, let me see if I can read your handwriting."

"Have you seen the new movie, _____? I think it's likely to be my favorite movie of the year. What's yours?"

Certainly none of these suggestions will electrify your companion, but they're all conversational leads — and the chances are that they'll lead somewhere rather than coming to a dead end.

YOUTH vs. AGE

That's all very well, you may say, when you're talking with people your own age. But what about talking to older people?

Your friend's parents probably read the same newspapers and magazines that your family do; they probably listen to the same radio programs and watch the same TV; they're probably interested in the same local, national, and international events. Use these topics as your starting point, but don't try to tell older people "what's what." Instead, ask their opinions. They'll be pleased and, no doubt, full of answers.

Fair warning: No matter whether your conversation partner is young or old, don't criticize or make disparaging remarks about other races or religions. And steer clear of political arguments unless you're on very friendly terms with the person you're talking to. Even so, it's better to warm up to a hot political discussion in your own home with your own family rather than when you're a guest elsewhere.

SHORT STOPS

At group gatherings among close friends, there's nothing more fun than discussions or even arguments. But don't make rash statements; you can't drive home a point unless you know facts. Steer clear of what can become unpleasant quarreling. Some of the danger signs are: raised voices, name-calling, interrupting the person who's speaking; making personal, rather than factual, remarks. When those signals start flashing, it's sensible to revert to nonsense:

"Whew! Settling the fate of the world is tough work. Let's take a break and get some dance music on the radio."

"Look, we're getting nothing out of this except hoarse voices. Anybody want to play a fast and silent game of ping-pong?"

OUCH!

There! You've done it again — put your foot in your mouth, and someone's feelings are hurt. How were you to know that Laura would walk in just as you were telling Agnes, "Oh, I'm sure of it. Laura told me very confidentially—"

The look in Laura's eyes tells you that now a friendship hangs in the balance — and all because you didn't stop to think before you spoke.

Here are some conversational faults to avoid:

Gossiping. Mum's the word. How can you expect people to trust you if you repeat what they tell you in confidence?

Criticizing adversely. Look for what's *right* with people rather than what's wrong with them. You'll find that in so doing you'll begin to like more people, and certainly more people will begin to like you.

Belittling. You're not going to be popular if you're always trying to "take someone down a notch or two" with expressions like "Huh, that's nothing." Try substituting, "Good for you!" or "Won't you show me how you did it?"

Ridiculing. Everyone finds himself in a ludicrous position at some time or another. Don't make fun of people until they see the joke on themselves. Then you can laugh *with* them.

Lying. You won't save any hurt feelings if you use the "little white lie" method of declining a date because of a "headache" and then that "headache" is seen sitting in the movie beside you! Better tell the truth and nothing but!

Boasting. Are you sure you haven't told that before? Are you sure other people want to hear so much about your achievements? If they had an equal chance to boast, you might find that their accomplishments really give you something to shoot for!

Sniping. Are you sometimes surprised to hear a nasty tone in your own voice? Do you "fly off the handle" and say things you really don't mean? Then hold your tongue — until you can speak calmly, clearly, and sincerely.

Telling embarrassing jokes. Don't tell jokes that might offend other people — and that means not only off-color jokes but dialect jokes and others that make fun of certain races, nationalities, or groups of people. Put yourself in the other fellow's shoes!

Always arguing. Discussion is a healthy thing but continual disagreement with other people, trying to prove that you're "an individual," is likely to leave you enjoying your own company — and who wants to argue with himself?

Domineering. Don't try to "run things." The happiest associations, friendships, and marriages are give-and-take, where nobody "bosses" and everybody shares.

TWO LITTLE WORDS

There are no more expressive and no more frequently-needed words in the language than these two twosomes:

"Thank you."

"I'm sorry."

The uses of "Thank you" run from little things, such as thanking a boy for holding open a door or helping a girl off with her coat, to spoken thanks for a gift, a party or dance invitation, a job interview, a pleasant occasion or entertainment.

The uses of "I'm sorry" run from a simple apology for bumping into someone or sneezing too close to someone to a statement of extreme regret for a serious mistake, misstatement, or hurt to someone else.

Don't be afraid to use these twosomes often — when you can do so sincerely.

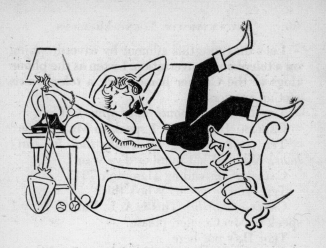

WHAT YOU SAY
. . . on the telephone

THE PHONE rings. You answer. What sort of impression do you make? Do you show symptoms of *telephonitis?* Do you gulp, mumble, bellow, or shriek? Do you snap, coo, or whine?

The point is that, on the telephone, *what you say* and *how you say it* represent YOU. Your voice and your words are stand-ins for your smile, your gestures, your personality — all the things people *see* when they talk to you in person. And you can't have "ear-appeal" if you suffer from *telephonitis.* Your social phoning will be awkward and your business calls inefficient.

Let's diagnose this ailment by eavesdropping on a telephone conversation. Listen as the phone rings at the Cramer home. Ted, a *telephonitis* victim, answers:

TED *(through a mouthful of apple):* H'lo.

CALLER: Hello. May I speak to Mr. Cramer?

TED *(still chewing so loudly that he can't hear):* Who? What number d'ya want?

CALLER: I'm calling Hampton 7945.

TED: You've got it. Who's this?

CALLER *(shortly):* This is A. L. Futrell. May I speak to Mr. Cramer, please?

TED: He's not here.

CALLER: Oh. *(Pause)* Thank you. Good-bye.

Unfortunately in this situation, what Ted doesn't know does hurt him. Let's see what might have happened if his telephone manner — and manners — had made a good impression on Mr. Futrell.

TED: Hello. Ted Cramer speaking.

CALLER: Hello, Ted. This is A. L. Futrell. May I speak to your father, please?

TED: I'm sorry, Mr. Futrell, my father won't be in until about eight this evening. May I take a message for him?

CALLER: That won't be necessary, Ted. We can discuss the matter. I called to ask your father if you'd be interested in an after-school job at my store.

TED: Why, thank you, Mr. Futrell. I certainly would be interested. May I stop at the store tomorrow afternoon about four to discuss it with you?

CALLER: That'll be fine, Ted. See you tomorrow.

TED: All right, Mr. Futrell. And thank you again. Good-bye.

AT HOME ON THE PHONE

Your telephone technique can be just as smooth as Ted's if your tactics are simple and direct.

Here's a check-list of *do's* and *don'ts*.

1. Be conscious of your voice and your diction when you're talking on the phone. Use a normal conversational tone, speaking distinctly and directly into the phone, with your lips about one-half inch from the mouthpiece.

2. Answer the phone in a brisk, cheerful manner. No drawling, no murmuring, no grumbling, no mumbling through chewing gum or food.

3. Identify yourself (or give the phone number) as soon as you pick up the receiver.

4. If your caller doesn't give his name, ask "Who's calling, please?" Don't risk the embarrassment of guessing incorrectly.

5. Give your complete attention to the person phoning. Finish any other conversation *before* you pick up the phone. And if you must interrupt a phone conversation say, "Excuse me a moment, please." (Never say, "Hold it!" or

"Hang on a sec!") Cover the mouthpiece during the interruption. When you go back to the phone, say, "I'm sorry I kept you waiting."

6. Treat wrong numbers politely: (if you're the victim) "I'm sorry, but you have the wrong number"; (if you're the offender) "I must have the wrong number. I'm sorry I disturbed you."

7. If you're the caller, be sure you have the correct number before you call. (Don't always trust to memory!) Even so, if the person answering doesn't sound familiar, don't bark "Who's this?" or "What number is this?" Politely ask, "May I speak to Lois?" or "Is this Oxford 4324?" And *never* be guilty of that childish game, "Guess who this is!"

8. Plan your calls so that they don't interrupt meals at the home of the person you're calling. To be safe, ask, "Is it convenient for you to talk now? If not, I'll call back later."

9. If the person you're calling isn't at home, leave your name, even if you don't leave a message. It's inconsiderate to be mysterious about your calls. (That goes double for a boy who calls to ask a girl for a date!)

10. When you can't hear the other person, it's simpler and safer to say, "I'm sorry, I can't hear you," rather than grunt, "Huh?" The latter often results in this sort of mix-up:

"Huh?"

"Whadyasay?"

"I said huh."

"Huh what?"

"Couldn't hear you, so I said huh."

"Oh!"

Make your telephone calls short and sweet. Don't be a hanger-on.

Start developing a simple and direct telephone technique by making a mental or written outline — before you pick up the receiver — of all the points you wish to cover during the call. Why are you calling Tina or Pete or the cleaner? How many things do you have to mention? Keep them all in order, and keep to your subject.

PHONING FOR A DATE

Let's say you're calling Janet Carr to ask her for a date for Saturday night. Both your family and Janet's will appreciate your keeping the conversation to this minimum:

MR. CARR: Hello. John Carr speaking.

YOU: Hello, Mr. Carr. This is Tom Bostwick. May I speak to Janet?

MR. CARR: Surely, Tom. I'll call her. Just a moment.

JANET: Hello, Tom. This is Janet. How are you?

YOU: I'm fine, thanks, Janet. I hope you are, too. I called to ask if you'd like to go to the movies with me Saturday night.

JANET: Yes, Tom, I'd be delighted. What time shall I be ready?

You: Will eight o'clock be all right? The feature begins at eight forty-five.

Janet: Eight will be fine. I'll see you Saturday. Good-bye, Tom.

You: Goodbye, Janet.

That was an easy one, of course, because Janet was cooperative and she knew that, when boy calls girl, it's the girl's place to end the conversation. (However, if she's a hanger-on, it's perfectly all right for the boy to sign off.)

Usually the caller is the one to lead into the good-byes, as soon as he has concluded the purpose of the call. That's a knack you should cultivate; it comes in handy when you have a long list of people to phone.

CALLING A CLUB MEETING

Let's say you're phoning about a club meeting. Before you start phoning, jot down all the details of the meeting — why it has been called, where and when it will be held. Then you'll be able to speak your piece quickly and clearly. Once you've heard the other person's reply, you're justified in using a quick windup — "Fine. Then I'll see you at the meeting. Good-bye." Very often that's the only way to forestall a resume of the week's activities.

TAKING MESSAGES

Keeping a pad and pencil near the phone is very important for the many times you'll have to say, "I'm sorry, my father (or mother or sister) isn't at home. But I'll be glad to take a message." And after you've jotted it down, ask, "May I read it to you, to be sure I've taken it down correctly?"

It's permissible for you to ask a friend's father or mother to take a message for you, if your friend isn't at home when you call — *provided* you can make it brief and understandable.

You have no right to expect anyone to follow a lengthy dispatch such as, "Please tell Chet that we'll meet him at the gym about a half-hour before the game, unless it rains and we don't go. But he'd better wait until eight o'clock before he leaves the house, because Sam may be able to borrow his father's car and then we'll drive over to Newburg instead of going to the game."

That certainly doesn't live up to the technique of being simple and direct.

GETTING DOWN TO BUSINESS

Large stores and offices usually have switchboard operators who route all incoming calls.

If, for example, you should be telephoning a large department store to report non-delivery of a purchase, ask the switchboard operator (the one who answers your ring with "Hahn's Department Store — good afternoon") to whom you should make your report. That's much easier than reeling off your story to a clerk only to find that you should have asked for someone in charge of complaints.

Once you get the right person or department, make your report as businesslike as possible — and be sure you have your facts straight.

YOU: I'd like to report the non-delivery of a tennis racquet purchased on Monday, May 10th, in the sporting goods department. It was promised for delivery by Thursday, May 13th.

STORE EMPLOYEE: I'm sorry. Was this a charge or cash purchase?

YOU: It was to be charged to Mrs. Henry Faulk and sent to Miss Diana Faulk, both of the address, 103 Wentworth Drive.

STORE EMPLOYEE: Thank you. I'll check on this immediately. May I call you?

YOU: Yes, my home number is Glendale 8054 — and I'm Diana Faulk.

STORE EMPLOYEE: Thank you. I'll call you later today, Miss Faulk.

YOU: Thank you. Good-bye.

LONG DISTANCE

Long-distance calls are either person-to-person or station-to-station. Both are toll calls and the telephone company makes a special charge for them. When you make a person-to-person call, there is no charge if the person isn't there. A station-to-station call means that you'll speak to whoever answers, and the charges are somewhat less than for a person-to-person call.

Try to arrange to place your long-distance telephone calls from your own home (where they'll be added to the monthly telephone bill) or from a pay station (in which case, have a variety of coins ready for deposit). Don't impose on your friends by expecting them or their parents to pay for your long-distance calls, even if the charge is slight — for example, on interurban calls between nearby cities. If you don't have a phone in your own home, be very careful always to repay the neighbor whose phone you use, both for long-distance and local calls, if there is a charge for local calls or if there is a limit on the number of calls at a regular monthly charge.

In an emergency, when you're calling your family or very close friends, you can ask the operator to reverse the charges. If the person on the other end of the line agrees, the call will be put on the receiver's bill.

When placing a long-distance call, tell the operator the name of the place you're calling, and the telephone number. (If you don't know the number of the phone, give the name and the address of the person in whose name the phone should be listed.) If you wish to know the charge for your call, ask the operator to let you know after the call has been completed.

Here's the way a person-to-person long-distance call might be made:

You call the long-distance operator.

OPERATOR: Long distance.

YOU: Operator, I'd like to put in a call for Middletown, Iowa — a person-to-person call to Mr. Tom Burke, who lives at 1040 Hill Street. The phone is probably listed in the name of Mr. H. M. Burke.

OPERATOR: Thank you. What is your number, please?

YOU: Rockville 4069, and it's listed in the name of my father, R. O. Cameron. Will you please let me know how much the charge is?

OPERATOR: Yes. Thank you. (She puts through the call.) Here's your party. Go ahead. . . .

Within a few minutes after you've finished your call, the operator will call you and report the toll.

This request for a report on the charges isn't necessary, of course, but it's wise to keep a record of such charges, particularly if you're one of a large family and there are frequent long-distance calls in your home. Why? The better to be able to answer the question, "Who's running up this telephone bill?" at a family budget session!

WHAT YOU WRITE
. . . in social notes and letters

"GOLLY, I suppose I'll *have* to write that letter!"

Does that have a familiar ring?

Then follows your mumbling and grumbling and fidgeting. Finally, you produce a duty letter that reads exactly like — a duty letter. Perhaps the recipient of your letter may be glad to get even a few dull words from you. But if you're taking the time and the trouble to write, why not make your letter add up to good reading?

How can you do it? First, by giving your attitude a "face lifting." Look at personal letter writing this way:

When you get a friendly (social) letter, you're pleased, aren't you? You're pleased that someone took the time to sit down and tell you news you wanted to hear.

The same thing is true in reverse. So in writing a friendly letter, you're trying to give someone else pleasure. That's your purpose.

LETTER PERFECT

In social letter writing, you have a choice of tools: pen and ink or a typewriter. (*Never* use a pencil for either social or business correspondence.) Typed letters are all right except when you're answering a formal invitation, writing a letter of sympathy to someone who's had a death in the family, or writing congratulatory notes. True, your typewriting must be clear and accurate. A poorly typed letter with rambling margins and crossed-out words certainly isn't a compliment to the person who receives it. Make your letters neat, even if you have to write them on scratch paper first and then copy them for the final draft.

Handwriting

Either blue, blue-black, or black ink should be used. (No rainbow effects, please!) And try to make your handwriting as legible as possible, even if it isn't graceful. You can make it readable if you write slowly and carefully and omit any fancy loops or swirls. Try also to keep

your lines straight — no uphill-downhill trails
— and your margins even.

Stationery

Choose your personal stationery as carefully
as you would a new blouse or shirt. White stationery is always correct; cream or pale gray
stationery is acceptable. If you prefer tinted
stationery (as some girls do), stay on the conservative side with soft shades of blue, green,
or pink, and with little or no ornamentation.

For girls and women: either single sheets or
four-page folders.

For boys and men: fairly large single sheets.

Sequence of Pages

The size and shape of the envelope determine
whether a single sheet is to be folded once or
twice for insertion. Either way, the writing goes
from top to bottom.

When a four-page folder is used for a short
letter, the usual practice is to start on page one
and finish on page three. For a longer letter,
you may use the regular sequence: one, two,
three, four—or go from one to four, then opening the sheet and turning it sideways, write on
the two pages as if they were one long page.

Since the first page is easily identified, it
need not be numbered, but play safe by num-
bering the other pages so your reader won't

have to go back and forth frantically searching for the end of a sentence!

ADDRESSING THE ENVELOPE

Either the block form or the indented (or slanted) form is correct for the address of the envelope. The Post Office prefers the latter, because it's easier to read quickly. (See illustration on this page.) Also, the Post Office prefers that the return address be placed in the upper left-hand corner of the front of the envelope.

(Small stickers with your name and address in print can be obtained from stationers or department stores at a nominal price and are convenient to use as your return address on envelopes and parcel post packages.)

Your name	Stamps and Delivery
Complete street address	Method
City, State	
	AIR MAIL, or
	SPECIAL DELIVERY,
	REGISTERED,
	FIRST CLASS, etc.
Name	
Room, Apartment, or Box Number	
Street Address	
City	
State	
Attention	
Division or Department	
Holding or Forwarding	
Directions	

Each person for whom the letter is intended should be listed. (The over-all term, "F. F. Fuquay and Family," is not considered correct.)

SPECIAL CASES

Envelopes addressed jointly to men with titles and their wives are written this way:

The Rev. and Mrs. Clement Carstairs
Dr. and Mrs. Edward Morgan

But the wives alone are addressed:

Mrs. Clement Carstairs
Mrs. Edward Morgan

An envelope to a priest is addressed: The Rev. Patrick O'Malley. But the salutation of the letter is Dear Father O'Malley.

In writing to a U. S. (or State) Senator, the envelope should be addressed: The Honorable (or The Hon.) Charles Carter, United States Senate, Washington, D.C. But the salutation is Dear Senator Carter.

In writing a member of the House of Representatives (or of a State Legislature) a similar form is followed. He should be addressed as The Hon. George Domino, House of Representatives, Washington, D. C., but the salutation is Dear Mr. Domino.

The same form is followed for women who are Senators or Representatives. Address the envelope: The Hon. Mary B. Hanna. The salutation is Dear Mrs. (or Miss) Hanna.

When writing to a widow, continue to address her by her husband's name: Mrs. Forrest Parks (not Mrs. Myra L. Parks, unless she is known professionally by this name).

Address divorcees by their married names until you can find out what their preference is. (Some revert to their maiden names; others use a combination of their maiden and married names.)

Use of Abbreviations

The Post Office urges that, in addressing envelopes, you write out words like Street and Avenue, as well as the names of states (in handwriting Me. and Mo. can look very similar); also, that you write the full name of the town or city instead of just the word "City." If you know the zone number, use it after the name of the city.

Chicago 22
Illinois

Or this way if you're writing in a small space —say, on a parcel post label:

Chicago 22, Ill.

Instructions

Instructions to the Post Office ("Air Mail," "Special Delivery," etc.) are written in the upper right-hand corner below the stamps.

Special instructions, such as "Please Forward" or "Hold for Arrival 9/14" (in addressing someone expected to arrive at a hotel), are written in the lower left-hand corner, but "Personal" and "Important" are not considered correct for social letters.

FROM BEGINNING TO END

The correct form for a social letter is:

1501 Caroline Drive
Houston, Texas
June 12, 19—
or June 12th (year optional)

Dear (or My dear) Sally,

Sincerely (or Affectionately or Devotedly or Lovingly) yours,
Pat

June 12, 19— or June 12th
(Optional placement of date)

Body of Letter

As to what comes in between "Dear Sally," and your signature, remember always to keep your reader's interests foremost in your mind. You wouldn't write the same thing to both your grandmother and a former classmate who's moved to another city. Grandma would rather hear about the family, whereas your former classmate would be more interested in school news.

Shock Absorbers

Be careful not to shock your reader if you have bad news. Don't start out bluntly: "Mother's in the hospital with a broken ankle." This is better: "Something happened yesterday that had us worried for a while, but now we're encouraged. Mother tripped on the lower step of the stairs and broke her ankle. Dr. Bramer thought it best for her to stay in Memorial Hospital for a few days. He says she's coming along fine and will be home this week end. She sends you her love and says to tell you not to worry. Dad and Bud and I are taking care of things at home. . . ."

Another warning: Don't leave your reader up in the air with only a vague clue to hang onto— such as, "Bud will get rid of his bandage today." (What bandage? Why? What happened?) On the other hand, don't go into minute details so that your letter reads like a horror comic. Give your reader the necessary information but don't linger over the unpleasant.

Handle with Care

Try not to be a gossip or a rumor-monger. And beware of putting into writing anything that might be considered unkind or damaging to someone's reputation if the letter should be read by a third person. (Letters are sometimes opened by the wrong persons or they may be carelessly left where a third person can see them.) If you're angry or resentful when you sit down to write a letter, better give yourself a cooling-off period and your letter a rewriting before you mail it.

Also beware of putting into writing any strong feelings of affection unless you're sure that the recipient of your letter feels the same towards you. Even so, remember that, particularly among teen-agers, feelings are likely to change frequently. Promises of undying love made one week or month may look ridiculous—even to the promiser—a few weeks or months later. It's safer to write friendly, newsy letters, concentrating on items that have meaning for the two of you.

If you're on the receiving end of a "love letter," remember that it was written to you and for you *only*. Never boast of your conquests by putting such letters on display. No matter what your feelings toward the person who wrote the letter, have respect for his or hers.

THANK-YOU NOTES

Thank-you notes are a "must" to show your gratitude for a gift, a special favor, or a week-end (or longer) visit in someone's home. Make them brief; make them sincere. Make the other person feel that his efforts are appreciated.

Here are some examples, which should be read, *not* copied. Your notes should express

your own personality just as much as your
clothes and your manner of speaking.

It's a Gift

> 600 South Main Street
> Ironton, Pennsylvania
> January 3, 19—

Dear Uncle Scott,

It was beginning to look as if that stream-
lined fountain pen in Lacer's window never
would be mine. Now, thanks to your Christmas
check, I'm the owner of a first-rate fountain
pen. You can see from this letter that I've found
an immediate use for your gift.

The family are all well, and we had a happy
time at Christmas, beginning with our usual
neighborhood carol sing on Christmas Eve and
ending with Mother's plum pudding on Christmas night. We missed you, though, and hope
you'll be with us next year.

Thank you again for your thoughtfulness.

> Affectionately yours,
>
> Arnold

When a friend of the family sends a ticket to
a play, concert, game, or some other public entertainment and you're the lucky one to use the
ticket, it's thoughtful of you to write a note of
thanks.

45 Prospect Road
Flint, Michigan
February 10, 19—

Dear Mr. Witherspoon:

What a happy surprise when Dad told me that you'd offered us a ticket to the professional tennis exhibition at the Armory last night! Since tennis is my favorite sport, I was the lucky one to attend.

All of the matches were well-played, but the men's doubles turned out to be the closest. The final set was the most exciting one I've ever witnessed.

I'm grateful for the opportunity to have seen such famous players.

Sincerely yours,

Bob Parnell

Invitation and Reply

When you're writing to invite a friend to visit you for overnight or longer, remember two things: Be warm—be specific. Let your friend know that you're hoping he (or she) will accept. Be definite about such things as time of arrival, and length of stay. You may also mention particular activities you're planning, so your friend will know what clothes to pack. (Or you may include that information in a second letter, after your invitation has been accepted.

Pine Lodge
Pineville, Tenn.
August 15, 19—

Dear Kit,

As soon as your duties as a camp counselor are over, how would you like to "get away from it all"? Pine Lodge isn't a very elegant cabin, but we can offer you mountain air, tennis, swimming, and a little peace and quiet after your summer with the "young fry."

Mother says that the Barbers, who have a cabin here, are going to be passing through your town en route to Pineville on September 2nd. I think you said you'd be home from camp by then, and they could pick you up and bring you here if you're able to come. Dad could drive you home on September 6th, when he leaves on a business trip.

I do hope you can come. I'm eager to see you after all these months, and I want to hear all about your fearful and wonderful experiences at camp. If your answer is "yes," Mother will write your mother about the arrangements with the Barbers.

Affectionately,

Sue

An invitation rates a quick "yes" or "no" reply. Details (how and when you'll arrive, if you accept) can wait for a second letter to your hostess. But you should let her know as soon as possible whether you can accept.

Camp Cherokee
Tryon, North Carolina
August 21, 19—

Dear Sue,

Yes, yes, yes! I'd love to visit you at Pine Lodge. I checked with Mother as soon as I received your invitation, and she's given me the green light. She also said that she thinks your mother is wonderful to be willing to take on a guest so near the time you close the lodge for the season. I think so, too.

At this point, I'm just as glad to think that I'll be leaving my little charges before long. But I wouldn't have traded this experience for anything. Maybe while I'm at Pine Lodge I can talk you into coming here as a counselor next year.

I'm looking forward to seeing you and your family again.

Affectionately,

Kit

Bread-and-Butter

After a visit in the home of a friend, you owe your friend a letter of thanks within a week after your return home, but first and foremost you owe your friend's mother—or the official hostess in the home—a word of appreciation.

> 265 Green Street
> Selma, Alabama

Dear Mrs. Watkins,

Thank you for having me as your guest last week end. I enjoyed every minute of my stay, and the buffet supper on Saturday night was an occasion I'll long remember. Mother says that, from my description, your Angel Food cake truly must be heavenly!

My parents join me in sending regards to you and Mr. Watkins.

> Sincerely yours,
>
> Neil Carr, Jr.

January 5th

CONGRATULATORY NOTES

You'll find many occasions for the writing of congratulatory notes. They range from birthdays and anniversaries to engagements to news of achievements, such as election to office, receiving awards, scholarships, or other honors.

Older people, in particular, are most appreciative of attention on their birthdays and other anniversaries. Although there are printed greeting cards for almost every occasion, there is nothing so personal and grateful as a handwritten note.

Birthday Greetings

> 21 Park Circle
> Marion, Indiana
> May 15, 19—

Dear Grandfather,

Happy, happy birthday!

I've just mailed you a small surprise gift to help you celebrate.

I'm so glad that you're my grandfather. Who else has a grandfather who can dance the polka on his 75th birthday anniversary?

> Your loving granddaughter,
>
> Irene

Engagements

The announcements of engagements are also occasions for the writing of congratulatory notes, and the rule is to wish the bride-to-be good luck and congratulate the groom-to-be.

142 Seaway Drive
Miami Beach, Florida
August 22, 19—

Dear Karen,

I'm so glad to learn that you and Peter are going to be married. He's a fine person, and I hope that you and he will make the ideal married couple.

We're all eager to know your plans. Have you set the date yet?

Sincerely,

Marvin

142 Seaway Drive
Miami Beach, Florida
August 22, 19—

Dear Peter,

Congratulations on your engagement to Karen! From all I've heard of her, she must be a wonderful girl. My best wishes to both of you for many years of happiness!

Sincerely yours,

Marvin

Achievements

Congratulations for achievements are easy to convey, in person, to friends you see frequently, but out-of-town friends deserve a note when you learn of some unusual achievement of theirs.

> 7654 Cayuga Drive
> San Pablo, California
> May 10, 19—

Dear Jean,

Tonight's *Evening Herald* brought the good news about you. Congratulations! It's a real achievement to be valedictorian of your class and I'm proud of you.

Will you be at the beach this summer? If so, perhaps we can go "crabbing" together again. At any rate, I'll hope to see you there.

> Sincerely yours,
>
> Laura

NOTES TO CONVALESCENTS

In writing notes to friends who are ill, remember that they've probably heard—and felt —more than they want to about what ails them. It's your job to cheer them up, so don't be guilty of writing a "weeping willow" note. Keep it gay —and put the emphasis on the person's recovery.

17 Hanover Place
Portland, Maine
October 4, 19—

Dear Fred,

Imagine spending two weeks at home with a good record player and a radio, not to mention having breakfast in bed and people waiting on you all the time! And with all the fan mail you're getting, you probably think you're a Hollywood star.

Seriously, Fred, we miss you and we're all hoping for your speedy recovery. When you're feeling fit again, we're going to organize an express service to your house to bring you daily assignments, library books, and the like. In the meantime, several of us are trying to take complete class notes so we can help you catch up.

Get well soon!

Sincerely,

Jerry

NOTES OF SYMPATHY

Notes of sympathy, when someone close to one of your friends has died, are hard to write. But they may be—and should be—brief. Just say what is in your heart, as simply and sincerely as possible. It isn't even necessary to use the sad words "death" or "died" in such a note.

695 Mesa Street
Phoenix 5, Arizona
March 25, 19—

Dear Harriet,

I've been thinking of you ever since I heard
the news. My heart is with you. If I can help
you in any way, won't you please let me know?

Sincerely yours,

Thelma

CHRISTMAS CARDS

Sending Christmas cards isn't a necessity; it's
a thoughtful, friendly gesture. Like anything
else, it can be overdone. If it becomes a chore
or a feverish effort to send as many cards as
Jane Jones sends, then the custom loses its
meaning. Your time could be better spent in
other ways and your money could be better
spent if given to some worthy charity.

Perhaps the best solution to the problem of
where to start and where to stop in a Christmas
card list is to favor those whom you don't have
a chance to greet often during the year. You can
say "Merry Christmas" in person to your family, your neighbors, your classmates, and many
of your schoolmates, but the friends who live
far away, or even those nearby whom you don't
see often, would appreciate your greetings on
a card. This is particularly true of older people

—relatives to whom you don't give gifts and friends of the family who have known you since you were a child. Take time to write them Christmas notes (a poinsettia or a star sticker centered at the top of a sheet of white paper can be Christmas stationery) or send them printed Christmas cards with personal messages added. The gesture will represent more than a few cents' investment on your part.

INFORMAL INVITATIONS, REPLIES

Inviting friends to an informal party can be done by phone or in person, but sometimes it's a better idea to write notes so that your guests will have the date firmly in mind. This is particularly true when you're issuing invitations for a party to be held during a festive season, such as Christmas.

R.S.V.P.

If it's important for you to know the exact number who will come, write R.s.v.p. (initials of the French expression, *Répondez s'il vous plait*, which means *Reply, if you please*) in the lower left-hand corner of your note. R.s.v.p. is frequently seen in social invitations, but if you think your friends won't understand what you mean, just write in the lower left-hand corner, *Please reply*.

144 Stratford Road
Seattle 7, Washington
December 8, 19—

Dear Tom,

Beware of the mistletoe, but do come to my house on Saturday night, December eighteenth, at eight-thirty o'clock. There'll be dancing to popular "platters" and other entertainment, too.

Sincerely,

Anne Merriman

Please reply

Acceptances

Here's a correct reply to such an informal invitation:

113 Church Street, N. W.
Seattle 3, Washington
December 10, 19—

Dear Anne,

I am looking forward to coming to your party on Saturday night, December eighteenth, at eight-thirty o'clock.
Thank you for inviting me.

Sincerely yours,

Tom Applegate

Regrets

And here's the way another person might send regrets:

> 6016 Third Street
> Seattle 7, Washington
> December 10, 19—

Dear Anne,

I'm sorry that I won't be able to come to your party on Saturday night, December eighteenth. My family and I are leaving on December seventeenth to spend the holidays with my grandparents in Tacoma.

Merry Christmas and a Happy New Year!

> Sincerely yours,
>
> Harry Halprin

CALLING CARDS AND "INFORMALS"

In years past, calling (or visiting) cards were in general use because the custom of making formal social calls was in vogue. Other uses for the calling card (approximately 2" x 3" in size and with the name engraved or printed) were for the writing of informal dinner or party invitations, for acceptances or regrets to such invitations, for enclosures with flowers, wedding gifts, and other gifts.

Because the custom of making formal social calls has practically disappeared, except in diplomatic and military circles, the use of the engraved or printed social calling card has decreased. (Name cards for business purposes are still widely used.) More popular today is the "informal," a foldover note with the name printed on the top outside fold.

On calling cards or "informals," girls usually have "Miss" placed before their names. When they write personal messages on the card, the "Miss" is crossed out.

FORMAL INVITATIONS

Formal invitations, usually engraved or printed, require *handwritten* replies in the same formal third-person language and in a form similar to the invitation (*not* in paragraph form, as informal replies are written). Write your reply in ink on white paper.

Here is an example of a formal invitation:

Mr. and Mrs. Henry Becker
request the pleasure of your company
at the Kent Hill Country Club
on Friday evening, January fourth
at nine o'clock

Dancing

R.s.v.p. to
9 Cedar Place

Here is an example of the wording and form of a reply:

> *Mr. Frank Salino*
> *accepts with pleasure*
> *the kind invitation of*
> *Mr. and Mrs. Henry Becker*
> *at the Kent Hill Country Club*
> *on Friday evening, January fourth*
> *at nine o'clock*

If you're unable to attend, you substitute for line two either of these:

> *regrets that he is unable to accept*
> *regrets that a previous engagement*
> *(or illness or whatever) prevents him*
> *from accepting*

Most church wedding invitations do not include R.s.v.p., but most wedding reception cards do. These must be answered formally, too, although the details of hour and place may be omitted:

> *Miss Teresa Pinckney*
> *accepts with pleasure*
> *Mr. and Mrs. Scott Brown's*
> *kind invitation for*
> *Friday, the fourth of June*

WHAT YOU WRITE
. . . in business letters

IN THE years to come, you'll probably have occasion to write many different kinds of business letters, but for the present and the immediate future probably your business letter writing will be mainly letters of approval or disapproval, letters of inquiry, letters of order and adjustment, and letters of application. All of these come under the heading of business letter writing and will be more formal than social letters.

STRICTLY BUSINESS

Business letters should include a complete heading (street, city, complete date) an inside address, (name of firm, organization, or person, address) and, generally speaking, a more formal salutation and closing.

Salutations

Common business-letter salutations are *Gentlemen,* when you're addressing a firm or organization, and *Dear Sir,* when you're addressing a person (such as Personnel Director) whose name you don't know. The salutation of a business letter is always followed by a colon.

Closings

Common closings for business letters are *Very truly yours, Yours very truly,* and *Sincerely yours.* A comma follows the closings of business, as well as social letters, unless "open punctuation" style is being followed.

Signatures

In writing signatures for business letters, it sometimes avoids confusion for a single woman to write "Miss" in parentheses before her signature:

(Miss) Helen Canby

However, most people assume that a woman who signs her name without either "Miss" or "Mrs." before it is single.

Married women may sign their business letters either of two ways:

Mrs. David Marcus
or
Mary Lamb Marcus
(Mrs. David Marcus)

The latter form is preferred, particularly if there is a joint bank account for husband and wife and the wife signs her checks "Mary Lamb Marcus."

Men never use "Mr." in signatures.

LETTERS OF APPROVAL, DISAPPROVAL

In writing letters of approval — or disapproval — to public figures (Congressmen, authors, columnists, movie stars, radio and TV performers, recording artists, and the like), to newspapers and magazines (in this case usually you'll address The Editor), be sure to tell *why* you like or dislike what has been done. This sort of criticism is much more helpful than just a general "rave notice" ("I think you're wonderful. Please keep up the good work!") or a general condemnation ("I think your program is terrible. I'm surprised that anyone listens."). Be specific, especially when writing to editors and performing artists. Name the article, short story, program, record, etc., you liked or didn't like.

Above all, don't be guilty of name-calling or "angry language" when registering disapproval. A calm, clear statement of your opinion will do a great deal more to accomplish your purpose than any amount of ranting.

Here's an example of a letter of approval:

1010 South Main Street
Clydeville, Ohio
October 16, 19—

Mr. Biff McCune
The Bandstand
Station WXYZ
Toledo, Ohio

Dear Mr. McCune:

Some of my friends from Clydeville High School and I listen to your *Bandstand* over Station *WXYZ* every Saturday morning from 10 until 12 noon. We usually gather at someone's house and have a listening session.

I play a trumpet in a small dance band, and am a great admirer of Frank Signorelli, whose recordings you sometimes play. In fact, I think that your selection of records — especially the Dixieland Jamboree recordings of Wild Bill Davidson and W. C. Handy — is very good. I'd like to hear more of these old records.

We appreciate the fine broadcasts that you give us.

Sincerely yours,

Hal Newcomb

LETTERS OF ORDER, ADJUSTMENT

In writing letters of order and letters of adjustment (or complaint), the same rule as that for letters of approval or disapproval holds true: *Be specific.*

When ordering, be sure to give complete information: quantity, cost, description of item — by number or symbol, if possible — where you saw the ad (if any), and how you intend to pay.

Here's an example of a letter of order and a following letter of adjustment (or complaint):

> 533 Grover Court
> Ogden, Utah
> April 18, 19—

T. Hallimer Company
85 Front Street
Salt Lake City, Utah

Gentlemen:

Please send me one dozen white, hemstitched, linen handkerchiefs at $7.00 per dozen, as advertised in the April 17 *Evening Star.* I enclose a money order for $7.00.

> Very truly yours,
>
> Eleanor Anderson

533 Grove Court
Ogden, Utah
April 29, 19—

T. Hallimer Company
85 Front Street
Salt Lake City, Utah

Gentlemen:

On April 18, I sent you an order for one dozen white, hemstitched linen handkerchiefs of the kind advertised in the April 17 *Evening Star*. The handkerchiefs were priced at $7.00 a dozen, and I enclosed a money order for $7.00.

I received this order yesterday (April 28), and discovered that only six of the dozen handkerchiefs you sent me were white. The other six were blue.

I am returning the six blue handkerchiefs by parcel post today and would like to have them replaced by white handkerchiefs, as I ordered.

Very truly yours,

Eleanor Anderson

In writing letters of order for several different items, it's a good idea to itemize them; also in writing letters of order, it's a good idea to repeat the name and address in the body of the letter, as insurance that the merchandise will be sent to the correct address.

> R.D. 2
> Herkimer, N. Y.
> April 2, 19—

Montgomery Ward
Albany 1, New York

Gentlemen:

I am enclosing a check for $35.93, for which I would like the following items:

Quantity	Item	Number	Price
1	Ensilage Form	84 A 7238 M	$ 5.49
1	Dump Hay Rake	87 A 5378 R	24.45
1	"Calfeeder" Weaning Pail	87 A 4825 M	2.10
1	Good Flock Feeder	87 A 368 M	3.89
			————
			$35.93

This order should be sent to
> Harvey Eckhardt
> R. D. 2
> Herkimer, N. Y.

> Very truly yours,
>
> Harvey Eckhardt

LETTERS OF INQUIRY

Here are two examples of the letter of inquiry. The first asks for information about college entrance requirements and a catalogue; the second asks about accommodations at a motel and requests reservations.

111 Sunset Drive
Great Falls, Iowa
February 14, 19—

The Registrar
Timmons State College
313 South State Street
Timmons 3, Iowa

Dear Sir:

Would I be qualified to enter your freshman class next fall? I have a "B—" average in high school and would like to work towards getting a B.A. degree.

Please send me a copy of your college catalogue. I'd like to have information about courses of study, tuition, cost of room and board, part-time jobs, etc.

Yours very truly,

Nora Hook

755 Oak Street
Richmond, Virgina
May 24, 19—

Grand View Motel
Skytop, Pennsylvania

Gentlemen:

Could you accommodate three other teen-age
boys and me for four nights June 19 through
June 22? We'll be attending the Young People's
Conference at Hill Manor during that time. We
plan to arrive by noon on June 19, departing
shortly after noon on June 22.

We would prefer to have accommodations at
your minimum rates.

Please confirm this reservation, quoting rate
and type of accommodation.

Very truly yours,

Mark Nevins

LETTERS OF APPLICATION

In writing letters of application for jobs, the
problem is to give your prospective employer
sufficient information but not to burden him with
your "life story." Here's an example of a letter
of application.

853 Edgemore Street
Little Rock 8, Ark.
March 19, 19—

Box 25
The Times-Post
1558 Commerce St.
Little Rock 4, Ark.

Dear Sir:

I should like to apply for the job of salesman, which you advertised in the March 18 *Times-Post*. It is my understanding that you want a high school graduate to do sales work for your hardware supply company.

On June 13, I'll graduate from Central High School, 405 North Avenue, Little Rock. At Central, I've majored in business and studied bookkeeping, typing, business English, and retail selling. During my senior year, I have been assistant advertising manager of the *Central News*.

Since September, I have been employed as a part-time sales clerk at Goodwin's Hardware Company, 56 Broad Street, Little Rock. My employer, Mr. Frank A. Goodwin, says that he will be happy to recommend me.

I shall be happy to report for an interview at your convenience. My home phone is 4212.

Very truly yours,

Clay B. Lobak

WHAT YOU DO
... at home with your family

"WHAT *are* 'at-home' manners?" you may
ask. "I'm not expected to jump out of
my chair every time Mom goes through the
room, am I — or to forgo the best part of my
lamb chop when the rest of the family pick up
the bones with their fingers?"

Of course not. But "informal" manners are
quite different from no manners at all! Remember when, in the foreword to this book, etiquette
is defined as "a way of showing that you're
thoughtful of the other fellow"? Well, at home,
particularly, good manners are exactly that. The
"veneer" side of courtesy counts for little;
considerateness, cooperativeness, dependability,

and a *pleasant dispositi⋯* the "Big Four" contributions expected of you.

More specifically:

DO *keep your room clean and uncluttered.* Nothing is more discouraging to Mom, when she brings in your laundry, than to find an unmade bed, a desk cluttered with papers, and your clothes scattered over every spare inch of chair and floor space. Your room, as your private domain, is also your responsibility. Remember that, and do a good job in the maintenance department.

DO *put things back where they belong — in any part of the house.* If you've borrowed the screw driver, return it to Dad's tool chest, Mom's scissors to her sewing basket, your own coat to the coat closet. It's irritating to have to hunt for "lost" articles, and just as irritating to have to constantly tidy up a constantly-cluttered up living room.

DO *respect the privacy of the other members of your family.* Knock before entering their bedrooms, and *never* barge into the bathroom without knocking. And, while on the subject of the bathroom, be careful not to monopolize it during rush hours (usually early in the morning, and before and after meals); be considerate of the hot water supply, if limited; don't borrow personal articles; always leave the wash basin neat and clean; and leave your laundry to soak *only* with Mom's permission.

DO *show up promptly at meal time.* This, together with a few cheerful topics for conversation, is all it takes to make Mom feel that her labors in the kitchen have been worthwhile — although a "Gosh, this is good!" upon occasion certainly wouldn't do any harm.

DO *help with the household chores — cheerfully and willingly.* Disappearing at dish-washing time just isn't good sportsmanship. And you won't be a "sucker," either, if you do *more* than your share of the menial jobs. If you volunteer to clean up the kitchen alone when Sis wants to catch an early movie, she'll do the same for you another time. And an unrequested car-polishing job from time to time is "good politics."

DO *listen to the suggestions and criticisms of your parents.* Remember that, in some areas at least, their experience is broader than yours, and that you can benefit by it. Talking back accomplishes nothing; talking *out* your problems and differences, on the other hand, accomplishes a great deal. Many families have found that a good way to do this is to organize a Family Council — where the whole family meets regularly to discuss problems, air "gripes," and make plans that will affect the entire group. Everyone has a chance to speak, as well as listen, and where differences of opinion crop up, the issue is decided by democratic vote. Mutual rights and responsibilities are adjusted in these meetings and, over a period of time, a regular Family

Council can become the core of a harmonious, well-adjusted household.

DON'T *borrow anything from another member of your family without first obtaining the owner's permission.* You know how *you* feel when you've agreed to play tennis with a friend, and dash home for your racquet — only to discover that your brother has "borrowed" it for the afternoon. And it's always when you're sure "Sis won't mind" that she really does!

DON'T *monopolize the phone, radio, or TV set.* If there are family conflicts in the TV-program department, talk them over calmly, and be willing to compromise in order to reach a peaceful solution. Perhaps you could all take turns as TV program-chooser, or let each member of the family do the deciding at certain hours or on certain evenings. And when you're playing records or watching TV, keep the "volume" low enough so as not to disturb any other family members who may be reading or talking at the other end of the room.

Above all, remember that, after a quarrel, you owe your fellow-family member an apology — just as if he were anyone else. And "Thank you's" and "Excuse me's" are just as important in your private life as they are in public.

In short, to get along with others in the best possible way, you have to be your best possible self. And isn't the happiest possible home a goal well worth working for?

WHAT YOU DO

... on a date

"WHATCHA doin' Saturday night?"

Hold it! That's how *some* fellows ask a girl for a date, but they're the ones who usually wind up spending an evening with the boys. Girls are allergic to guessing games. "Gonna be busy Saturday?" and "Guess who this is?" are telephone tactics that leave the ladies cold. Even the most eager girl is strongly tempted to answer "Yes!" to the first question, and "I don't care!" to the second. And *no* girl likes to admit that she's "doing nothing" Saturday night!

So put the question to her straight. It doesn't matter whether you write, phone, or "pop the question" in person. But however you do it, don't hem and haw. Don't apologize: "The movie at the Center probably isn't very good, but. . . ." If you want a date, say so, and tell the girl exactly what you have in mind:

"The new Danny Kaye picture is coming to town next week, Liz. Would you like to see it with me Saturday night?"

or

"Would you like to go to the square dance with me Saturday night, Gail?"

If you have no special plans in mind, your best bet is the honest old standby:

"How about a date Saturday night?"

It's that simple. Granted that none of those opening lines is exactly inspired, but neither is "Yes, I'd like to!" And that's all *you're* hoping for, isn't it?

As for you girls, a direct question deserves a direct answer. Yours should be either "I'd like to go," or, "Sorry, but I've already made plans for Saturday." No stalling, please. If it's a house rule that you check with one or both of your parents before accepting a date, explain the situation frankly, and tell your would-be date that you'll let him know as soon as you can. Then follow through. If you keep him dangling for longer than a day or two, he's likely to think you're waiting for a more exciting invitation. And if he does, it'll be a long time before you hear from him again!

Beware, too, of the temptation to manufacture an alibi when you'd rather not go out with a certain boy. "Other plans" will cover anything from another date to shampooing your hair. So stick to that formula, and don't invite trouble by telling Joe, for instance, that you'll be "out of town this week end." You and Joe just might show up at the same dance *in* town this week end. Such things have been known to happen, much to the embarrassment of the "out-of-towner"!

HERE YOU COME!

Once you've landed a date with a girl, your next move is to land on her doorstep — on time. And a horn-honk in front of her house is no substitute for a handshake with her parents in the living room.

Don't be surprised if you have to hold your own with your date's family for a few minutes. Even the loveliest of lassies sometimes manages to be upstairs putting the finishing touches on her hairdo when you call for her. But even if she's a "dream come true," who is ready on the dot, it won't be wise of you to make a dash for the front door without giving her parents a chance to look you over.

Your date's parents aren't going to ask for your credentials or put you through the third degree. All they want to know is whether you're the sort of boy they'll be proud to have their daughter date — and they'll make mental notes of your appearance (spic and span?), manners (standing until both Mr. and Mrs. Blank are seated), and whether you can carry on an intelligent conversation (ask their opinions and let them do most of the talking).

Many boys make the mistake of slighting parents in their public relations policy. But a little courtesy in the Parents' Dept. will go a long way at some future date when your girl is angling for a special late permission.

THERE YOU GO!

"Where to?" This can be an embarrassing question, unless you know your date well, and don't mind deciding "where" together on the spur of the moment. Even then, it's usually a better idea to have your plans formulated in advance, so she won't have to worry about what to wear. And *you* won't have to rule out bowling, because she's "too dressed up."

Especially on a first date, you should choose your entertainment carefully. If you're shy on conversation, a movie is a good bet. You're sure to have the film as common ground — i.e., as a conversation-starter — at the Soda Bar afterwards. Attending ball games or other sports is even better. You can chat when you please, or concentrate on the game almost entirely. If there's a teen hangout in your town where you can dance and play ping-pong, as well as talk, that would be a good choice. The same goes for school mixers, bowling, and listening to records at a friend's house.

Take your choice. Or you might make several suggestions and let your date choose the entertainment. But whatever you do, plan in advance as much as possible. Try to limit any last-minute "Where to?" to something like a choice between movies — "Shall we see *Desperate Journey* or *Lover Boy?*" — and make no major changes in previous plans without consulting your date first!

BEST FOOT FORWARD

If you like Jane well enough to ask her for a date, you'll naturally want to impress her, too. And that takes more than just a well-scrubbed appearance and careful date-planning. More than the "gift of gab," too. The ladies are sticklers for small courtesies.

Of course, girls can put on their own coats and open doors for themselves. But they appreciate the thoughtfulness of boys who instinctively perform these small courtesies for them. So keep your eyes open for occasions to be of service — until these gestures come naturally. And cheer up! It won't take long.

Along with coat-holding and door-opening, your date expects another consideration from you, and a much more important one: *that you get her home on time.*

Aim for a little on the early side, just to be

safe. She'll be as sorry to see a good evening come to a close as you will, but she's the one who'll have to face the family fireworks if she doesn't meet her curfew. And remember: Extra prompt service this time will prove that you're a reliable fellow for future reference.

If you're delayed, your date should phone home to explain the situation — but even then only a real alibi will excuse you to her folks.

Since your date may feel embarrassed about telling you that eleven o'clock is the dating deadline in her household, better ask what time she'd *like* to be home before you start out on your date.

WIND-UP ITEM

Don't make the mistake of presuming that all dates have to end in a big clinch — or even a little hearty hand-holding. Girls distrust a boy who's a "grabber"; boys don't stay interested long in an "easy number."

Who's to know? Well, you don't think that those lively discussions in the boys' and girls' locker rooms center around the latest crisis in world affairs, *do you?*

MORE DATING DATA

Blind Dates — are no breach of etiquette *if* they're arranged by a friend. And they needn't be totally "blind," either, if said friend is neither blind nor deaf to your likes and dislikes. Of course, if you're expecting to meet a Hollywood glamour girl or a TV singing star, you'd better stay at home with your pin-ups. But if you're looking forward to meeting an average teen-ager — like yourself — you probably won't be disappointed. And if you put your best foot forward, he (or she) will probably do the same.

If you should get "stuck," though, be on your best behavior anyway. Even a calculated risk backfires sometimes, but that doesn't cancel your contract. And even if it doesn't lead to a beautiful friendship, one evening isn't an eternity!

"Blind dates" generally work out best as half of a double date combination, where everyone present already knows at least one other member of the foursome. Under no circumstances should a girl accept a "single date" invitation from a total stranger. That would not only be foolish, but dangerous.

Smoking and Drinking — If you know your family disapproves, it would hardly be "cricket" of you to accept a cigarette or an alcoholic beverage when you're on a date. So if you should ever find yourself in a group where cigarettes or cocktails are being served, you should say "No, thank you" as a matter of course.

You don't have to make an issue of it. You don't even have to say "I don't smoke" or "I don't drink." Just "No thanks" is enough. People don't sit up and take note if you by-pass a chocolate, do they? Of course not. So treat cigarettes and whiskey the same way.

If the others *insist* that you take a drink or a cigarette, stick to your guns, but pass it off lightly and with a smile: "No. Really." Or, if you're asked "What'll you have?" when the people you're with are ordering cocktails, just say cheerfully, "One ginger ale — straight, please." That way, you'll be sticking by your principles without being "prudish."

Girl dates Boy — The general rule is that it's up to a boy to ask a girl for a date. However, there are two notable exceptions:

1. A girl may invite a boy to her club dance, a "Sadie Hawkins" party, or to any bring-your-own-date affair to which all the girls are asking boys. She should, however, explain this to the boy when she invites him, so he won't feel embarrassed about accepting. If he does accept, the girl, of course, foots the bill for the evening.

2. A girl may invite boys to a party to which she's asking a number of both boys and girls.

Boy-girl Gifts — Gifts from boys to girls, and vice versa, shouldn't be either (a) too expensive or (b) too personal. A girl should be especially careful not to give a boy a present at Christmas, for example — that's more expensive than his to her; nor should she be the first giver. Except for a "steady" or a very old friend, she'd do better to stick to an especially-shopped-for Christmas or birthday card. They're always appreciated, and it's the gesture of thoughtfulness, not the gift itself, that counts.

Anyone can give gifts. The art comes in fitting the gift to the person. And this takes more headwork than pocketbook. Jenny, who's a sailing enthusiast, would rather have a simple bright bandana than a bottle of expensive perfume. Mike, who likes folk singers, would rather have one Richard Dyer-Bennett record than an album of some popular singer. And, to sweet-toothed Elliott, a batch of homemade cookies would be the best gift of all.

So, come your next gift-giving time, make a list of the receiver-to-be's hobbies, tastes in reading, and your mutual interests. That way, you should hit on an idea that will please *both* of you.

THE IDEAL DATE

Here's a check list for daters. See how you measure up.

The Ideal Date (boy) —

. . . asks for a date at least a few days before an informal affair, two weeks to a month before a formal dance.

. . . is well-groomed and appropriately dressed for the occasion.

. . . is courteous and sincere — no "line," please.

. . . never deserts his date for another girl.

... doesn't talk about other dates to the girl he's with.

... is a good listener, as well as a good "talker."

... doesn't act loud and boisterous; doesn't swear.

... respects his date's abilities and opinions, knows girls aren't all "fluff."

... has a sense of humor.

... can take "No" for an answer.

The Ideal Date (girl) —

... is ready when her date calls for her.

... is attractively and appropriately dressed.

... is natural and sincere; doesn't "put on airs."

... doesn't flirt with other boys or talk about other dates.

... doesn't apply make-up in public.

... is considerate of a boy's wallet.

... never breaks a date for a "more attractive" offer.

... when asked for what-to-do or where-to-go suggestions, has a few up her sleeve.

... can keep up a conversation.

... is enthusiastic, doesn't save "Thank you's" for a canned curtain speech.

WHAT YOU DO

. . . at parties and proms

"GOODBYE, Jo — and thanks for a *wonderful* party!"

"That goes for me too, Jo."

"Thanks a million, Jo. Best party I've been to all year."

" 'Night, Jo. It's been the greatest!"

Then suddenly the last guest has gone. The party is over. And it's time to write the happy ending: *A good time was had by all.*

A good time. That, of course, is the goal of any party. But, unfortunately, things don't always turn out that way. Such as:

1. The party that takes a painfully long time to get started.

2. The party that slows down after an hour or so, and never perks up again.

3. The party where some show-off insists on monopolozing the spotlight, thus ruining the fun for the rest of the crowd.

Let's stop there. You already know that the list of party-fizzlers is practically endless. You want to know how to *avoid* such mishaps, and how to cure them — and pronto! — when they do pop up.

YOUR ROLE AS PARTY HOSTESS

To earn the reputation of a "hostess with the mostest," you'll need to combine two ingredients — planning and practice. Only by planning a party carefully can you be sure of coming up with exactly the right blend of guests, activities, and refreshments. And only through practice at party-giving can you achieve that apparently effortless knack for "keeping things rolling" — the trademark of any Hostess First Class.

For easy planning, let's divide the rules into a "before, during, and after" series.

Before a Party

1. For an informal party, invite your guests about a week ahead of time by phone, in person, or by note. In any case, remember to include the three "musts": date, time, and place of party.

2. If the party is to be a co-ed affair, you may either invite all your guests individually, or ask the (boys or girls) to bring their own dates. The ask-everyone-yourself method is usually preferred because then your company is less likely to pair off permanently into pre-determined couples. And, of course, it's all right for a girl to invite any boy she knows to a "mixed" party, whether he's ever dated her or not.

3. Plan to serve refreshments that can be prepared the night before, or simple ones that can be quickly assembled. A hostess should have fun at her own party, but that's almost impossible if she has to spend a large part of the evening in the kitchen.

4. If dancing is to be the evening's chief entertainment, be sure that your record player is in good working order, and that you have a sizeable selection of dance records on tap. Borrow as many extra platters as you can, of course, but be sure they're returned to their rightful owners at going-home time, or at least by the following day.

5. If you plan to devote a lot of time to playing games, make a long list of them. Most games begin to drag after twenty minutes or so, and it's far better to be ready with too many than to have too few possibilities on tap.

During a Party

1. Greet your guests as they arrive, and show them where to leave their coats. Stay near the door so the new arrivals won't have to search for you, and introduce any "strangers" to a couple of the "old-timers" right away.

2. Your parents should be at home, as official party chaperons. They can retire to the den or their bedroom for most of the evening, but they should be on hand at least to meet and greet your guests as they arrive. Even if Mom and Dad trust you to run things with no assistance, your *guests'* parents probably expect at least one adult to be present, and you owe it to them to stick by convention. Besides, your parents' presence is excellent emergency insurance. Should gate-crashers appear, Dad can get rid of them for you. And disaster in the kitchen? Mom to the rescue!

3. Divide your attention equally among your guests. Make a point of seeing that everyone has someone to talk to or something to do at all times.

4. Come going-home time, be where your guests can find you — i.e., near the door. Don't embarrass them by apologizing for any mishaps which may have occurred. When they thank you for the party, just smile and say, "I'm glad you could come."

5. And if a guest doesn't know when to leave, ask him to help you clean up! (This fix can be

avoided, though, in one of two ways: Let your
guests know *when you invite them* that your
party is "from eight to twelve"; or get your best
friend to start off the exodus when the witching
hour arrives.)

After a Party

1. Leave every room and everything you've
used or borrowed in good condition.

2. Show your parents that you appreciate
their permission to give a party by doing something extra nice for them.

PARTY PROBLEMS

If a guest "won't play," ask him to be captain
of a team or to take a prominent part. (This is
99 and 44/100 per cent sure.)

If a guest is a "show-off," give him a chance
to perform — your way. Let him go first in a
story-telling or stunt session, or encourage him
to run through his "prize performance" quickly
for the entire assemblage. If he begins to monopolize the party, turn up the music and announce an elimination dance, or play another
game.

If a guest is unusually shy, make him feel
necessary. Let him pass the nuts, hand out the
pencils, etc. And maybe you can round up a
sympathetic guest to try to "de-shy" him.

If gate-crashers arrive, tell them as tactfully
as you can that you'd like to be able to invite

them in, but there just isn't enough room. Of course, if a good friend drops in solo, by accident, it would be nice of you to ask him in — and leave it up to *him* to bow out of the situation gracefully. However, if the party-crashers are real, numerous, and persistent, you'd better send out an S.O.S. to your parents. Dad will send them hustling in no time!

YOUR ROLE AS PARTY GUEST

When you accept an invitation to an informal party, you owe it to your hostess to arrive as close to "starting time" as possible. As soon as you arrive, greet your hostess, her parents, and any guest of honor — *before* joining your special friends at the other end of the room.

The ideal guest is gay but not boisterous. He falls in with whatever his hostess suggests, helps out where he's needed, and is genuinely interested in his fellow guests. If he's urged to perform, he does so without being coaxed, and he's a good sport about "coming across" when a game requires that he pay a forfeit.

When there aren't enough chairs to go around — and there rarely are in a crowded room — a boy should offer his seat to any girl who stops to chat with the group he's in. The girl accepts readily and graciously. She doesn't say, "Oh no, thank you" — unless she's *really* moving on right away. And in that case, she should add pleasantly, "I'm looking for Val Drake" — or whatever her reason is for not remaining.

If you should accidentally drop, spill, or break something, apologize to your hostess, do what you can to clean up the "spillings," and then try to forget the matter. Should you break an article of any value (a flower vase, perhaps, or a serving platter), a private offer to replace it would be appreciated. But prolonged apologies or an agonized attitude will only put a damper on the party.

Leave at the time specified on your invitation, or heed any "party's over" cues from your hostess. If you must leave early, just thank your hostess (explaining why you must go), say good-bye to the people nearest to you — and leave. No long-winded "I'm *so* sorrys," please. And naturally, no matter when or with whom you depart, a "Good-bye and thank you" to your hostess (and her parents, if they're in the room) is in order.

PROM NOTES

What to Wear. If the prom is "formal," boys wear dinner coats ("tux") and black ties; girls wear evening dresses. If the dance is "semi-formal," the girls wear formal gowns — either full-length or ballerina — and the boys wear dark suits (usually navy blue). Girls may wear evening wraps, but usually wear sports coats over their prom dresses. Long evening gloves, worn indoors, are too sophisticated for most teen-agers, and the outdoor kind are meant to be worn *outdoors only*.

Corsages. Flowers aren't always a "must," but they are one of the "extras" that make a prom a red-letter day in a girl's date book. And if you can afford it, one of the nicest things you can do for your "Prom Queen" is to buy her flowers that harmonize with the color of her dress.

Choosing the right color is very important. If you take a chance on red roses, it's likely that your lady will turn up dressed in pink or orange. (Eek!) So ask your date either what kind of flowers she'd like or simply what color dress she'll be wearing. And don't be afraid that the first question will bring forth a demand for an orchid! Girls can add, too! When you ask your date what kind of flowers she'd like, she'll probably make a suggestion that leaves you some leeway in both cost and selection.

Prom-bound. Although girls are usually glad to ride in buses or subways or on trolleys when you haven't a car, try to arrange some other method of transportation on prom night. Evening dresses are apt to be fragile; they weren't designed to be worn in buses. So you might drive to the dance — in the family car, or with a group of friends, or in a taxi. Or your date might be able to come with friends, and you could meet her at the dance — on time.

Arriving. When you arrive at the dance, your

first stop is at the cloak-rooms—one for the boys, the other for girls — where you leave your wraps and give your appearance a final going-over. And, girls, if you would be loved by your dates, leave any feminine paraphernalia you may have with your coat! No boy likes to lug his date's compact, handkerchief, scarf, etc. around in his pockets all evening. Those precious pockets were meant to look sleek!

The Receiving Line. At most school proms, there is a receiving line at the entrance to the dance floor — composed of the dance committee and the faculty chaperons. Don't "duck" the line. Go down it — boy following girl — introducing yourself (and your date, if he or she is not from your school) to any chaperon you don't know (or who doesn't know you). And smile as if you meant it! After all, there wouldn't *be* any prom without the chaperons.

You should also make it a point to thank the chaperons when the prom is over. And, although you don't *have* to ask Mrs. Dibble to dance, she would undoubtedly be pleased if you did so. And, who knows? Her samba might be just as flawless as her geometry!

Exchanging Dances. Proms may be program dances (each girl has a formal program with a dancing partner listed for each dance), exchange dances (the girl dances with her date except for either planned or impromptu exchanges with other couples), or cut-in dances (a girl starts dancing with her date but there are a sufficient number of "stags" present so that she gets many cut-ins). At any prom, a boy usually dances the first dance, the last, and the numbers just before and after the intermission with his date. The rest of the time, he is responsible for seeing that she's never left stranded, but otherwise he's on his own. You are *not* expected to dance every dance with your date. She'd like to "whirl" with many partners, and the more you can help to provide her with, the merrier.

Even before the prom, you might ask Chet, Bob, and Alan to trade a dance apiece with you. Then spot them on the floor, and you're all set. Besides prearranged exchanges, though, introduce your date to the friends you meet *at* the dance — the refreshment table is a good spot. After a four-way conversation over a cup of punch, it's the most natural thing in the world to suggest changing partners for the next dance. And, especially if she's a stranger in town, your date will appreciate your thoughtfulness.

Asking for Dances. At program and exchange dances a boy asks a girl to dance simply by approaching her and saying, "May I have this dance?" *Never* ask, "Is this dance taken?" — because no girl likes to admit that it isn't. At any private dance — school dances included — you may ask any girl to dance, whether you've been "officially" introduced or not. Self-introductions aren't only accepted; they're expected.

A girl replies to a boy's invitation to dance by saying either, "Yes, I'd love to," or, "I'm sorry. I've promised this dance." She never says "No" to one boy, and then dances off with someone who asks her later. If she refuses a dance without having promised it earlier to another boy, she owes it to her rejected partner to "sit this one out." If she accepts, she leads the way to the floor, and the dance is on!

Cutting-in. A boy "cuts in" on a dancing couple by walking across the floor, and tapping the dancing boy on the left shoulder. "May I cut in?" he asks. (It is rude simply to demand, "Cut!")

The boy "cut in on" immediately relinquishes his partner to the newcomer, thanks the girl for the dance, and leaves the floor. He never "cuts back in" on the boy who "cut in" on him. If he wants to dance with the same girl again, he must wait until she has a new partner.

At a private dance, a girl never refuses to dance with a boy who "cuts in." No matter how much she regrets the interruption, she must accept his compliment graciously. And she should be grateful for so much attention!

When "stuck." A boy need never "get stuck" with a partner if, at the end of a number, he takes her back to where he found her, thanks her, and leaves. Or, if he's still "unrescued" after several dances, he can still take her back, thank her for "the dance," and leave. He should never, however, leave a girl stranded in the middle of the floor.

A girl may excuse herself from a long-term partner and repair to the powder room for a few minutes before returning to the floor — and a new partner. Or she might suggest "sitting this one out," and introduce the boy to some friends by the refreshment table. It is her privilege, and hers alone, to suggest leaving the floor in the middle of a dance. Without her signal, the boy must "on with the dance" until the music stops.

WHAT YOU DO

. . . at the table

YOU'RE giving a dinner, and it's your party — from beginning to end. You've invited nine friends — four girls, five boys — to dinner on the evening before school reopens after summer vacation. The idea: to launch the new school year with a bang. The plan: Your family will eat before the guests arrive, then stay on the sidelines — except for, perhaps, your younger brother (or sister), who has been pressed into service as a waiter. But aside from your "outside help" in the serving department, you, as hostess, are in complete charge of the whole affair. And you want it to be pretty special — a real *dinner party*, not just a buffet supper.

Once you've issued the invitations (by note, in person, or by telephone), your course of action should be as follows:

A DINNER PARTY

Your first concern is the menu for your dinner. The food should be easy to eat *and* to look at; it should also be simple to serve.

Fruit Cocktail
Chicken and Rice Casserole
Peas and Mushrooms
Tomato and Lettuce Salad
Rolls   Butter
Ice Cream and Chocolate Sauce   Cookies
Coffee

In this case, you'd plan to have the fruit cocktail on the table when you and your guests enter the dining room. Then your "waiter" would remove the empty dishes, and serve the main course and salad. The casserole, which you would have prepared that morning, would be warming with the rolls in the oven during the first course. And the peas would be timed to simmer atop the stove until serving time.

Getting Set

A dinner table may be set in a number of ways, but it should always be pleasant to look at. Either a tablecloth or place mats may be used. A centerpiece is not necessary if the table is small and likely to be crowded, but it always adds a nice extra touch — *if* it's low enough not to obstruct the fellow across the table! Silver, whether it's stainless steel or sterling, should be gleaming. Glasses and china should also be clean and sparkling. (If the family "party" glass and china has not been recently washed, it's a good idea to wash it the afternoon before the dinner.)

The placing of silver and dishes at each place follows standard rules. The following diagram shows where plates, silver, and glasses are correctly placed:

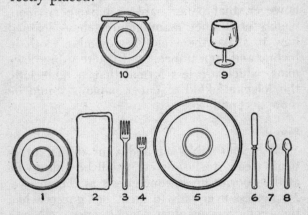

1. Salad Plate. 2. Napkin. 3. Fork. 4. Salad Fork. 5. Plate. 6. Knife. 7. Dessert Spoon. 8. Teaspoon (for Cocktail). 9. Glass. 10. Bread and Butter Plate.

You should set your table well ahead of party time. Put the napkins to the left of the forks, because in this case the fruit cocktail will be on the plates when your guests come in. However, when you are having no first course, or are planning to have it brought in after the guests have been seated, you may put the napkins on the plates, if you prefer.

If you're using a linen tablecloth, use linen napkins, if possible, even though you don't look forward to having to wash them out after the party. Paper napkins have a way of suggesting that the hostess is more interested in saving herself work than in pleasing her guests. It's true, however, that paper napkins have been more widely used since manufacturers have learned how to make them closely resemble cloth in feeling and appearance. So if you're using place mats, which are less formal than a tablecloth, the "elegant" kind of paper napkins would be quite acceptable.

Places!

With your table set and your dinner practically ready to be served, you'll be able to be at the door to greet your guests as they arrive. No hostess ever fails to greet her guests when they come in, nor does a guest ever walk into another room before he has spoken to his hostess.

Lead your guests into the living room, to sit

and chat until everyone has arrived. (*Note to guests:* It's all right to be as much as fifteen minutes late when you've been invited for dinner at a certain time — but never later than that!) Soon after the last guest has arrived, suggest that you all move into the dining room.

You lead the way to the dining room. Following you, the boys either accompany their "dates," or stand aside to let the girls enter first. For parties of eight or more, it's a good idea to put place cards at each place, alternating boys and girls. However, if you don't use place cards, your guests should wait for you to tell them where to sit. Then the boys seat the girls on their right before sitting down themselves.

The Meal Begins

After everyone has been seated, pick up your outside spoon and begin to eat your fruit cocktail. (The general rule is to use *outside* silver first, working inward as the meal progresses.) The others, who will wait for you, as hostess, to take the first bite, will then do the same.

Your "waiter" will clear away the cocktail cups and underlinings when all the guests have finished eating. He may remove each guest's dishes from either the *left* or *right* of the guest. However, any dish that is presented to a guest must be presented from the *left*.

Only two dishes should be removed at a time

— one in each hand. Stacking dishes as you remove them from a table is o-u-t, even if it does save time.

When the waiter has removed all traces of the first course, he brings on the next. Using the menu suggested, he would serve the casserole first, the peas next, then the rolls, and, finally, the salad. Or he might set the casserole on the table before you, and put the peas and mushrooms in a covered dish to your right — in which case *you* would fill the dinner plates and pass them to your guests, in turn (girls first, then boys). Your amateur waiter would then have only to pass the rolls and the salad.

Normally, no one should begin to eat until everyone has been served and you give the starting signal by picking up your own fork. But if you do the serving from the head of the table, and if there are a great many "mouths to feed," you should ask your guests not to wait. Hot food will sometimes get cool if everyone waits until the serving has been completed, and it would be a shame if your guests couldn't sample your casserole at its best!

As hostess, your job is to see that all of your guests enjoy the meal. This means that you keep a watchful eye to be sure that your guests have the necessary silver (although a guest may request a piece of silver if he's faced with the task of eating a main course with a spoon).

—and Then Dessert

After everyone has eaten his dinner — and perhaps you, as hostess, have suggested "seconds" and served them—your waiter removes everything from the table except the water glasses and dessert silver — and the centerpiece, of course! He removes crumbs from the table and refills the glasses, then brings in the dessert. It would probably be easiest to place the dessert before each person individually — the ice cream in a stemmed dish, with a cookie or two on the plate on which the ice cream dish is resting. The chocolate sauce may be already on the ice cream, or passed by the waiter so that each guest may help himself.

At a formal or semi-formal dinner party, coffee is usually served either with the dessert or later in the living room. Preferably the cups should be the small (demitasse) size, with small (demitasse) spoons on the *right* side of each saucer, near the handle of the cup. However, regular-sized cups and spoons may be used. The coffee should be served black, as this is the way people usually drink after-dinner coffee, but a thoughtful hostess will have sugar and cream on hand anyway — for the guest whose tastes may *not* be usual. It is always more important to please your guests than to stick strictly to a rule or custom.

Whether you leave the table before or after

the coffee, it's up to you, as hostess, to make
the first move to rise. At the end of the meal,
wait for a quiet moment, then suggest that you
all adjourn to the living room. The boys then
help the girls from their chairs, and everyone
follows you into the next room.

A BUFFET SUPPER

A successful buffet table requires careful
planning. Everything necessary for the meal
must be on it — food, dishes, silverware, napkins,
etc. Since the guests will be walking around the
table in a line as they serve themselves, things
should be arranged in logical order. Butter, for
example, should not be at one end of the table
and rolls at the other. A guest who passed up
butter because he saw nothing that required it
might have to go back to the beginning of the
line to get his butter once he discovered the
rolls.

The buffet table *opposite* is planned so as
to present an attractive appearance and make
it easy for the guests to serve themselves:

There are, however, no set rules as to where
particular items must go on a buffet table. So
long as they are conveniently arranged, they
may go almost anywhere. Just keep in mind the
area of the table where the guests will start to
serve themselves. The dinner plates, silver, and
napkins should go there. And be sure, too, that

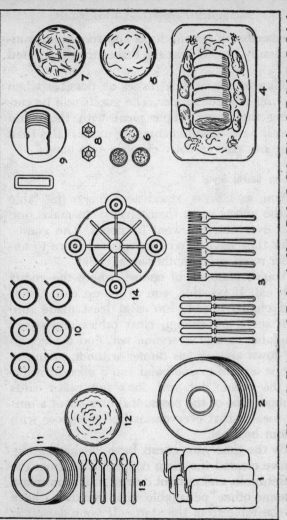

1. Napkins. 2. Plates. 3. Knives and Forks. 4. Main Dish. 5. Side Dish. 6. Relishes. 7. Salad. 8. Salt and Pepper. 9. Bread and Butter. 10. Beverage. 11. Dessert Plates. 12. Dessert. 13. Dessert Silver. 14. Centerpiece and Candles.

the necessary serving forks and spoons are conveniently placed near the dishes they'll be used for.

Plan to use as few dishes as possible when serving a buffet supper. The guests will be carrying their own whole meal with them and they'll have trouble managing more plates than they can conveniently carry in two hands!

Eating Buffet Style

You, as hostess, stand near the buffet table as the guests serve themselves — to make sure that everyone has what he needs. The guests, after they have filled their plates, retire to another room, or to another area, to eat.

You've planned, of course, where the guests will eat. If possible, you've set up card tables and chairs. If not, you've at least made sure that there are enough clear tables and chairs available so that everyone will find a place to sit down and eat his dinner without having to juggle a plate in one hand and a glass of water in the other. But you don't put place cards around. One of the pleasant things about a buffet meal is that everyone is free to choose with whom he'll eat.

By the time your guests have finished eating, you've cleared the main course dishes from the buffet table, and put out dessert, if it's ice cream or some other "perishable" that you didn't have on the table from the start. (If your dessert is cake, fruit, or something else that won't be affected by standing, there's no reason to wait to place it on the table.) Unless your guests have already discovered the new offering on the table, you move among them, asking them to help themselves when they are ready.

A FAMILY AFFAIR

When you invite a friend to dinner at your home with just you and the family, you are still, of course, your guest's hostess, but your mother assumes the role of Hostess-in-Chief. It is she who announces when dinner is ready, and who assumes the lead in the department of table signals. Your role is to help your guest "follow the leader" as graciously as possible. So don't make it hard for him (or her) by bouncing up from the table without excusing yourself, or by tackling your chicken before everyone has been served.

Also, when you've invited someone to "dinner with the family," it isn't likely that you'll want to "put on" an affair that's very different from your usual dinners at home. Certainly, you shouldn't by-pass any family table customs simply because you've invited a guest to dine with you. It's up to the guest to fit into your family circle for the evening, not up to your family to adjust to what may or may not be his method of procedure.

Saying Grace

Saying grace before meals is a custom in many households, and, of course, shouldn't be eliminated just because an "outsider" has joined the family group for dinner.

Since grace is usually said after everyone is seated at the table, and a guest waits for his hostess' cue before picking up his napkin under any circumstances, there is little chance of your friend's making a blunder when you're about to say grace.

However, if you know that your guest is of a different religion from yours, it would be thoughtful of you (or whichever member of your family says grace) to say a grace which is acceptable to *all* religions — like this very simple and familiar one:

> For what we are about to receive,
> Lord, make us truly thankful. Amen.

Or perhaps you'd like this one:

> We thank Thee, Father, for
> Food we eat, clothes we wear,
> Health and homes and friends. Amen.

TABLE MANNERS

Some people go after food the hard way by holding forks as if they were spears, knives as if they were daggers! For scooping up food, hold both fork and spoon handles like a pencil, in your right hand (unless you're left-handed,

of course). For steadying a piece of meat, hold
the fork handle in the palm of your left hand
and point the prongs down into the meat, using
the index finger as a lever. After you've cut the
meat, you may convey it to your mouth, as is,
or you may change your fork to your right
hand.

Hold the knife handle in the palm of your
right hand for both cutting and spreading (butter on bread, for instance). And don't try to
saw your way through a piece of meat.

When not in use, knife and fork are placed on
the right outer rim of the plate (but firmly, so
as not to slide off when the plate is moved), and
the spoon, bowl up, in the saucer or on the
plate. None of your silver should be left hang-
ing off your plate, gangplank style.

Even if you have strict instructions at home
to fold your napkin after a meal, you don't do
the same when you're away from home. As a
guest or in a restaurant, you aren't expected to
be back for the next meal. Your napkin is left,
unfolded, to the right of your plate.

Careful, Now!

Table manners involve a lot of "don'ts." For
that reason, they sometimes seem complicated
and unreasonable. But the real reason behind
most table "don'ts" is a good one: to avoid of-
fending other people. If you make noises while
you eat, attack your food so as to leave your

place messy, or pick your teeth, you're interfering with other people's pleasure in their meal. Good table manners, like good manners in general, add up to nothing more than consideration for the feelings of others. If you keep this fact in mind, your table manners are likely to be acceptable even though you don't know all the rules. But the following check list of "don'ts" can serve as a valuable guide.

DON'T play with your food. When you pick up a piece of silverware, you have one purpose in mind: eating. It's poor manners to sit — absently pushing your peas around while you're talking or listening.

DON'T chew with your lips open. Take small enough mouthfuls so that you don't have to.

DON'T put your elbows on the table while you're eating. You may rest your elbows on the table between courses, but never while you're eating.

DON'T cuddle a plate! Have you ever seen anyone eat with his left arm protectively encircling the plate? Then surely you know how bad that looks. Plates are to be eaten from — not hugged.

DON'T make objectionable noises at table. If you must blow your nose, do so quietly. If you swallow something the wrong way and begin to choke or cough violently, leave the table. (In a case like this, you needn't excuse yourself.) And never, never, let your eating be heard!

Don't guzzle soup or smack your lips. Don't choose a moment of quiet to begin chomping on your celery — wait until there are other distracting noises of conversation.

DON'T spit anything out. If you get something into your mouth that must be removed (bones, stones, etc.), remove it quietly. Use your thumb and forefinger, and choose a moment when no one is looking. If what you have taken out is unsightly (a spoiled clam, for example), try to cover it with something like celery leaves when you put it on your plate.

DON'T take your silverware from your plate when you pass your plate up for a second helping. The silverware you've been using remains on your plate, to one side.

DON'T push back your plate when you've finished eating. That gesture suggests that you're either eager for the next course, or eager to leave the table.

DON'T dunk. Even if you do like to dunk your doughnut in your coffee, it's still considered bad manners.

DON'T put liquid into your mouth if it's already filled with food. The food in your mouth should never be seen. If you drink with your mouth full, the food you're eating will be visible when you open your mouth to drink.

DON'T sop bread in gravy with your hands. It's all right to sop bread in gravy, but here's the way to do it: Put a piece of bread in the

gravy in your plate, then eat the bread with
knife and fork.

DON'T "stir" your food. Suppose you've been
served creamed chicken on a patty shell, with
rice to one side, and you want to eat the rice
and chicken together. *Don't* mix the rice with
the chicken on your plate. Take a small forkful
of chicken, put it into your mouth, and then
take a forkful of rice.

DON'T tip your dinner dish. If you want to
get those last few peas, tipping your dish so that
they fall together in the grove isn't the way to
do it. Use your knife as a barricade instead, and
push the peas against it with your fork. You
may tip soup or dessert dishes, *if* you tip them
away from the spoon instead of toward yourself.

DON'T bend over your plate. People who
eat with their heads bowed over their plates
seem to be concentrating on their food and ig-
noring other people at the table. Keep your
head up, so that you bring your fork to your
mouth instead of your head to the plate.

DON'T blow on your food. If it's too hot for
you to eat, wait until it cools off a bit.

DON'T butter a whole piece of bread at
once. Break off one piece of bread at a time,
butter it, and then eat it.

DON'T reach across another person for something you want. If the salt is to the left of your

left-hand dinner partner, never reach in front of him for it. Ask him to pass it to you.

Problem Foods

Some foods are harder to eat than others. Here's what to do when you're served —

Artichokes. Pull off the leaves one at a time, and dip the yellowish base in the sauce or butter that's been served with them. You eat only the tender base — pulling it through your teeth with your fingers to get the soft part out. Discarded leaves are placed to the side of your plate. If there are many of them, you may use your butter plate. When all the leaves have been picked off, you eat the bottom, or heart of the artichoke. You cut this heart in bite-size bits, and dip them into the sauce with your fork.

Bouillon. If this thin clear soup is in a cup, you may drink it from the cup — or sip it from a spoon, as you prefer.

Chicken. Broiled and fried chicken are eaten with fork and knife, when you're at a dinner table. When you're on a picnic — that's when using your fingers is in good taste.

Corn on the cob. Don't butter the whole ear at once, but butter as you eat. Eat about two rows of kernels at a time, and try to look as little as possible like a dog attacking a bone.

Fruit. Eat fruits like apples, oranges, plums, etc., with a fruit knife — cutting off segments of the fruit one at a time, and putting them into your mouth with your fingers.

Oysters and clams (half shell). Hold the shell steady with your left hand and, using an oyster or cocktail fork, loosen the oyster from the shell, then remove it all in one piece, if possible. Dip it in cocktail sauce (if an individual container is provided), and eat it in one mouthful. Oyster crackers may be dropped whole into the cocktail sauce and lifted up with the fork or they may be eaten dry, using the fingers.

Potatoes (baked). If you like the skin, cut the potato with knife and fork, and eat skin and potato together in bite-size sections. If you don't like skin, eat the potato right from the skin — scooping it out with your fork. Don't scoop out all the potato at once, and set the skin to one side.

Spaghetti. Spaghetti is easiest to eat when served with a large soup spoon. Hold the spoon in your left hand, almost perpendicular to the plate. Use your fork with the tip of the prongs against the spoon to wind the spaghetti into a bite-size portion. If you have no spoon, cut the spaghetti with your fork and eat it with the fork. You may eat the sauce that remains in the plate with a spoon, or drop small pieces of bread in it one by one, and eat with a fork. *Don't* let long lengths of spaghetti trail from your fork so that you have to hold the fork over your mouth and "feed" the spaghetti in.

WHAT YOU DO

... in a restaurant

WHEN you take a girl to a restaurant for dinner, your first move is to size up your surroundings. (It's a good idea to have made some previous investigation as to whether its prices fit your pocketbook.) Pause for a moment just inside the entrance — but out of the way of incoming traffic — and look around you. At the same time, take off your hat and coat.

Is there a checkroom? If so, you check your hat and coat. (If not, take them into the dining room with you and hang them on a hook or rack near the table.) Perhaps your date would like to have you check her coat too (ask her!) but most likely she'll prefer to wear it to the table

and — with your help or that of the waiter's or
the headwaiter's — drape it over the back of her
chair. If she's wearing a hat, she usually keeps
it on throughout the meal.

"TABLE FOR TWO"

Is there a hostess or headwaiter, or do you
have to fend for yourselves? If there *is* a headwaiter, it's his job to find you a table, so don't
just march in and sit where you choose. Wait
for him to come to you. When he does, ask for
"A table for two, please." Then he leads the way
to a table, your date follows him, and you bring
up the rear.

However, if there is no headwaiter, you take
over. Ask your date if such-and-such a table
suits her, and when she agrees (or, perhaps,
suggests another spot), you lead the way across
the room. And, since there is no one else to do
the honors, it's also up to you to hold your
date's chair for her and to help her remove her
coat.

A boy and girl normally sit opposite each
other at the table. However, you may sit on
your date's left, if you like. Just be sure you
offer her the seat facing the most pleasant view
— *not* looking into the kitchen.

Your date will probably keep her pocketbook
and gloves in her lap during the meal. If her
bag is cumbersome, though, she may put it on

an empty chair at the table, or even store it under the table. "No parking" on the table!

ORDER, PLEASE!

Once you're settled at a table, you turn your attention to the menu, which will be provided by either the headwaiter or the waiter for your table. If, as sometimes happens, no one pays any attention to you, don't get frantic, but don't wait until your date turns green around the gills. After a few minutes, beckon to a passing waiter, and say, "Will you ask the waiter for this table to bring us a menu, please?"

The correct way to order your dinner is, in itself, very simple. When the waiter comes to take your order, you ask your date what she'd like to eat, then you relay both orders to the waiter: "We'd like two fruit cocktails first, please, then one creamed chicken and one baked ham." Where your choices differ, give your date's order first.

If you'd like the waiter to describe or explain any item on the menu before you order, don't be afraid to question him. He'll be glad to help you decode those foreign words and phrases. This way you won't risk either missing out on a delicious new chicken concoction — or being horrified when the *escargots* you so suavely ordered turn out to be snails!

You may order your dessert at the same time

as the rest of your dinner, or wait until after the main course. Diners-out usually prefer to wait, though. A dessert that sounds "about right" before you start eating may look gargantuan after you've eaten the main course.

COUNTING THE COST

When you take a girl out to dinner, you should be prepared to spend more money than you would on a movie-and-soda date. Also, you should be careful to choose a restaurant where the prices aren't too steep for your wallet. Still, most restaurants offer dinners in a fairly wide price range, and it may be necessary to order carefully if you're to stay within your budget. Here are a few tips on how to keep the situation under control:

A formal dinner menu is usually divided into two sections: *table d'hote* (pronounced TAH-bul DOTE) and *a la carte* (pronounced ah lah CART). If you order *a la carte,* each dish will be charged for separately at the price listed on the menu. This not only makes it hard to estimate the total cost in advance, but also usually turns out to be the more expensive method of procedure.

Advice to budget-watchers: Concentrate on the *table d'hote* side of the menu. There you order from a list of complete dinners, and the entire meal — from appetizer to dessert — costs the amount listed beside the main dish, or *entree* (pronounced AHN-tray). One look will tell you what you can afford and what's "out of bounds."

True, a fellow can't hand-pick his date's dinner for her — but he can give her a good strong steer in the right direction! Instead of holding your breath and praying that she won't "break" you by choosing a sirloin steak, suggest a menu, within your price range — *before* she speaks up. For, example, you might remark, "This place is famous for its fried chicken," or, "That seafood platter sounds good, doesn't it?" A considerate girl will follow your cue and choose something at about the same price, even if it isn't chicken or sea food.

Note to girls: If your escort doesn't drop a hint, and the menu covers everything from hamburger sandwiches to filet mignon, it's up to you to do some tactful probing of your own. Don't assume that "the sky's the limit." On the other hand, don't decide dolefully, "Er, uh, I guess I'll have a hamburger." Find the happy middle way. Ask your date how a certain dish sounds to him — or if he recommends anything in particular. Or, when he asks what you'd like to eat, you might reply, "I haven't decided yet. How about you?" He *has* to come up with something then!

DURING THE MEAL

Once you've ordered, your meal should proceed smoothly. Your best table manners are a "must," of course, but this holds true whether you're dining in *or* out. There are, however, a few simple rules to bear in mind when you're eating in a restaurant:

First of all, if you need or want anything, ask your waiter for it. He's there to supply everything from more water to a missing fork, so don't hesitate to take advantage of his services. But don't yell, "Hey, you!" or practice your French with "Garcon!" to attract his attention. If you can't catch his eye, or if he doesn't seem to be around when you need him, quietly ask another waiter, "Will you please tell our waiter we need soup spoons?" And regardless of whether it's you or your date who needs the waiter's services, it's you, as the host, who should do the talking.

If you should upset something on the tablecloth, signal your waiter and quietly ask him to do any necessary cleaning up.

If someone you know stops to speak at your table, you should rise and remain standing for as long as he (or she) remains. Your date should stop eating, but she needn't stand up except for a much older woman. Usually a passing friend won't stay for more than a few words, but if he (or she) does, you should offer him (or her) a seat. If there isn't an extra chair at your table, ask the waiter to bring one.

You should rise, too, if your date excuses her-

self from the table during the meal — and help
to reseat her again when she returns.

Note to girls: Don't be embarrassed to ask
your waiter or any other attendant, "Will you
please direct me to the Ladies Room?" If there
is a woman attendant in the Ladies Room and
you require any unusual service or use a linen
towel (when paper towels are also available),
it's customary to tip her 10-15 cents.

PAYING THE CHECK

Sometimes the waiter will leave the check on
the table when he brings your dessert, but if
he doesn't, you should ask for it when you're
ready to leave: "May I have the check, please?"

When the check is brought, don't treat it as
the problem of the ages, but *do* check the
charges. Many a harried waiter has been known
to make mistakes, and a protest is certainly in
order if you find you've been charged for the
steak consumed by the gentleman across the
aisle! So review the addition as nonchalantly as
you can, but do review it. And don't hesitate to
ask about any item listed that you don't understand.

Your date, of course, doesn't look at the
check. Money matters are strictly between you
and the waiter.

If the waiter presents the check on a small
tray or plate, you're supposed to pay him. So
put the money on the tray with the check, and

add ten to fifteen per cent of the total bill for the proper tip. Or wait until the waiter brings back your change and then give him the amount of the tip.

However, if the check appears minus tray, look for the words, "Please pay cashier" printed across the bottom of the check. If they aren't there, ask the waiter, "Do I pay you?" If so, do so. But if the cashier is the person to be paid, leave the waiter's tip on the table just before you leave, and pay the check on your way out. (You'll have no trouble in finding the cashier; she's the most efficient exit-watcher alive!)

Is the waiter on hand to help your date with her coat? If not, that's your job.

Your date leads the way to the exit. She waits quietly to one side while you pay the cashier and claim your things at the checkroom. A dime or fifteen cents for the hat-check girl is your last obligation. Then you open the door for your date — and you're on your way!

DOUBLE DATES, PARTIES, AND "DUTCH"

When dinner in a restaurant is part of the plans for a *double* date, there are a few extra pointers to master:

When entering and leaving, the two girls lead the way, and the boys follow. (The correct order is *not* girl-boy-girl-boy.)

The waiter will probably seat one of the girls, and help her remove her coat. But he can't be

in two places at once, so it's up to one of the
boys to assist the other girl.

The girls sit across the table from each other,
their dates on their left — unless you're in a
booth. In this case, the two girls should always
sit on the inside.

To avoid a long and sometimes embarrassing
discussion when the check appears, it's generally a good idea for the boys to work out a
financial agreement ahead of time. Let one boy
pay the bill, the other settle with him later.

Party Pointers: If you should ever give a
luncheon or dinner party in a restaurant, be
sure to call up and make your reservation in
advance. Give your name, the number of guests
you'll have, and the time you expect to arrive.
If you'd like a certain table location, say so.

If the restaurant is new to you, check at the
same time on whether there's a cover charge or
a minimum charge. A cover charge is a set
charge per person in addition to the cost of his
meal. A minimum charge is the smallest amount
that will be charged each person — no matter
how little he eats. If you wait until it's time to
pay before finding out about these things, you
may be in for a shock!

You may want to serve a certain meal to all
your guests. If so, talk over the menu with the
manager or headwaiter at the same time you
make your reservation.

When you arrive at the restaurant with your

party, give your name to the headwaiter. Follow him to the table, preceding your guests — so that you'll be there first to tell them where to sit.

If you haven't chosen a menu beforehand and the group is small (4-6) you should ask your guests, in turn, what they'd like to have, then relay the order for the whole group to the waiter. If it's a larger group, ask the waiter to take each guest's order — yours last. And, as the host or hostess, the check, of course, is all yours.

Dining "Dutch": When two or more people are dining together in a restaurant, but each is to pay for his own meal, it's a good idea to ask the waiter for separate checks. Do this at the beginning, when you order. And, in this case, each person orders for himself.

When everyone's meal *is* included on the same check, though, settle the bill as quietly and as quickly as you can. The smoothest procedure is for each person present to pay his share to one member of the group, and to let "the treasurer" pay the cashier or waiter. (It's too much to expect the waiter to have to keep track of five different amounts of change for one check!) If your group can't settle your accounts quickly and easily at the table, try to arrange it so that one person pays the check, the others to settle their debts with him (or her) later.

WHAT YOU DO

. . . in public

YOUR public is watching!

Do you realize how true that is — that once you leave your own home, you're in the public eye, no matter where you go? On the street, in a car, at school, on the bus, at the game, at the movies, in church. Even if you just cross the street for an evening of TV at Chuck's house, you're "in public" while you're on your way.

ON THE STREET

Don't block traffic by walking more than two abreast on a narrow sidewalk. Passers-by want to pass by!

Don't chew gum, shout to your friends, or walk with your arm draped around someone else. Such things make you conspicuous, yes, but attractive, no.

A boy walking with a girl walks on the "outside" — that is, the side nearer the curb. (When he's with two girls, he may walk either between them or on the outside.) After crossing a street, he may have to change sides in order to stay on the outside. This he does by stepping behind the girl while she, in turn, moves toward the inside.

A boy guides a girl across streets by putting his hand under her elbow or by offering her his arm. Easy does it, though. No girl likes to be pushed or pulled through the streets.

If while walking on the street, someone with you stops to speak to another person, you walk on slowly unless you're called back for an introduction. If you're the one who has stopped to speak to another person, don't linger unless you do call your friend back for an introduction. And be sure not to block traffic while you're talking. Move to one side — preferably away from the curb — so that you won't be in the way of other people.

If he's wearing a hat, a boy always lifts it when he stops to speak to a girl or woman — even if he's merely returning a dropped package to a total stranger. He also lifts his hat if the girl he's with stops to speak to anyone on the

street. Hat-lifting occurs twice per stop — first,
with a boy's "Hello," and again when he says
"Good-bye."

ON A BUS

A girl boards a bus before her date does, but
the boy gets off ahead of her. This is so he can
help her alight — and also catch her pocketbook,
scarf, or gloves, should they fall.

If the bus has a rear exit, use it. Don't leave
by the front door, blocking the way of the people getting on. And if there is only one door,
consider who has the right-of-way. Stand aside
to let people off before you climb aboard.

Have your fare ready when you get on. Naturally, a boy pays both his own fare and his
date's, but a girl who accidentally meets a boy
she knows at the bus stop should not expect him
to pay her fare. If he insists, though, she should
let him pay. Such a small amount isn't worth a
traffic-blocking argument. The girl stands aside
while the boy takes care of money matters
and waits for him. If the bus is very crowded,
though, it's better for her to move back and let
him join her later.

As a "healthy young thing" in a crowded bus,
you should be glad to offer your seat to an older
person who is standing — especially to a woman
accompanied by a small child. And, sweet Sue,
if a husky Hank beside you stays right where
he is, that's all the more reason for you to offer

your seat to an elderly person. Hank deserves to
be embarrassed when you do!

Last but not least, a bus is no place for boisterousness. Besides dangerously distracting the
driver and annoying your fellow passengers, you
might miss your stop!

AT THE MOVIES

If you want top rating as a date, find out beforehand what time the feature starts, and plan
your arrival at the theatre accordingly. Your
date will appreciate seeing the beginning of the
picture before the grand finale!

When you arrive at the theatre, you buy the
tickets, while your date waits in the lobby, or
at least a few steps away. Unless there's a long
line — and a long wait — outside, she shouldn't
stick too close to you during the business
transaction.

Inside the theatre, after you've surrendered
your tickets to the man at the door, ask your
date "how far back" she'd like to sit. If there's
an usher, you relay her choice to him: "About
halfway down, please." Then the usher leads
the way to the seats, your date follows him, and
you're the caboose.

However, if there is no usher, you lead the
way to the seats, standing aside at the end of
the row to let your date enter first. On a double
date, you may sit couple by couple, or with the
two girls in the middle. Of course you say "Ex-

cuse me" to anyone you disturb — and be sure
to add "I'm sorry" if you step on toes.

Your date removes her coat as soon as you're
seated, and you help her arrange it over the
back of her chair. (You've already removed your
own coat in the lobby, and you hold it in your
lap during the picture — unless the theatre isn't
crowded and there's an empty seat beside you.)

If anyone enters your row, you rise to make
room for him to pass. Your date may remain
seated, if she can make enough room by pulling
in her knees. Otherwise, she stands up, too.

A girl removes her hat in a theatre, unless
she's *sure* it's so small that it won't bother anyone behind her. Even so, it's thoughtful of her
to turn and ask the person behind her: "Does
my hat bother you?" If a woman in front of you
is wearing a hat which blocks your view, ask
her politely, "Would you please take off your
hat?" Then thank her when she does so.

During the showing of the film, sit quietly.
Don't whisper, rattle candy papers, loudly
munch popcorn, or make sarcastic comments
about the action on the screen. And don't sit
with your heads together, or drape yourself over
an adjoining seat. Even if the movie bores you,
others may like it. Give them a chance.

IN CARS

You should never, of course, drive without a
license; and you should always obey the traffic

regulations of the community you're driving in.
(This includes not throwing trash out the windows!) Courtesy to pedestrians and other cars
is a "must" — for your own safety, as well as the
other fellow's peace of mind.

Don't pick up hitchhikers. There are laws
against this in many states — for your protection. If you trust your own judgment as to who
looks "safe," you're inviting disaster.

Avoid overcrowding a car. Crowds lead to
boisterousness, and boisterousness leads to accidents. Besides, the driver needs room to maneuver — *and* a clear view through the rear
window.

If you use the family car, be careful of it, and
considerate of your parents' needs. Let them
know ahead of time when you'd like to use the
car; replace the gasoline you used on that long
trip to Cedar Springs last Saturday. That's not
only good manners, but good politics!

In a car, a girl sits on a boy's right — unless
she's driving. The boy opens the door for her,
and closes it when she's safely inside. And, come
getting-out time, he alights first, then walks
around the car to open the door on her side.

In heavy traffic, however, the girl alights by
herself on the side near the curb, her date following through the same door. And when they
return to the car, she should suggest that he get
in first, from the curb side.

AT SCHOOL

Abide by the traffic rules in the corridors. Keep to the right; no shoving, running, sudden stops, or changes of direction. And several hundred locker doors slamming at once would mean bedlam, so keep it low!

Help keep the building clean. Students who carve initials on desks, write on the walls, or scatter trash about are being *expensively* inconsiderate. (Do you know who has to pay the cost of replacing desks, painting walls, etc.? Taxpayers — your parents!) Try, instead, to spare a few seconds to *pick up* papers, and turn in stray articles to the Lost and Found Dept.

Cleanliness is the rule in the rest rooms, too — the *only* places where you should indulge in hair-combing and lipstick-applying. Take your turn at the mirror quickly and quietly. The folks behind you have classes to make, too!

In the classroom, be sure to introduce any visitors to your teacher. And pay careful attention to what goes on; it'll save time later — for both you and Miss Garrett. No snickering, clowning, or notepassing. And raise your hand; don't wave it wildly.

When a class is over, resist the impulse to bolt with the bell. Wait for Miss Garrett to dismiss you. Anyway, if you skip out before she has time to give the assignment, you're just inviting a double dose of homework tomorrow.

Teachers are human, but they have a job to do. How easy (or hard) it is depends, to a large extent, on you.

If your school has a cafeteria, wait patiently in line for your turn to be served, and choose your lunch quickly so the line won't be held up. Be considerate of your neighbors at the table, and clean up your debris when you've finished — to save someone else the chore.

In the library, respect the "Quiet" signs and, when you must speak at all, keep your voice down to a whisper. Learn to depend on the card catalogue as much as you can; it will save the librarian a lot of needless effort. When you really need her help, though, try to take up as little of her time as possible, and thank her for her assistance. Above all, faithfully abide by the library rules, and handle any books you use or borrow *carefully*.

AT THE GAME

Good sportsmanship isn't reserved for the players on the baseball diamond or football field. Spectator sportsmanship is just as important as the attitudes of the players themselves. Loud booing and flying pop bottles at school games have a ruinous effect on a school's reputation. You know that there's no place for a jeering section in the cheering section, that umpiring is the umpire's job, and that the visiting team deserves a courteous reception

So give a "welcome" cheer to your opponents, and if one of their players is injured, cheer him, too. Above all, whatever the game's outcome, be a good sport. If you lose, admit that your team was outplayed, not "outweighed." If you win, celebrate, of course. Raise the roof for old Central. But don't let your enthusiasm take the form of "crowing." The losers know who won, too.

For girls only: If you're invited by a boy to a football game, and don't know the difference between a quarterback sneak and an end run, better bone up on the rules — ahead of time. You don't have to fill yourself to the bursting point with technical knowledge; just get acquainted with the rudiments of the game. Although Slim will be glad to answer a question or two, no boy enjoys explaining every play to his date. So learn enough about the game at least to be able to cheer in the right places. You'll not only be a better date for Slim, but you'll enjoy the excitement that much more for yourself.

IN CHURCH

Women and girls wear hats and gloves to church. Men and boys wear hats only in orthodox Jewish synagogues.

As for church customs, you're "at home" in your own church, of course, but visiting a friend's church is likely to be confusing. You expect to find the same reverent atmosphere there as in your church, but aside from that, you're not sure of anything. Here are some tips:

Where do you sit? If you are with friends who are members of the church, you'll no doubt sit with them. Otherwise, an usher will probably seat you. Although there are no "reserved pews" in church, some families have occupied the same pew for years, so you should be careful about "sitting anywhere" — especially toward the front of the church. You may, of course, ask to be seated in a friend's pew. But if there is no usher, it is usually safest to choose a pew near the rear.

Do you follow the service? In most churches, when you're visiting you may participate in the service if you like. If so, follow the leadership of someone nearby who seems to be familiar with the procedure. However, a visitor may sit throughout the entire service without participating, if he prefers.

Should you take communion? Unless the minister specifically invites visitors to take communion, you should not do so, but remain in your pew.

What about the offering? Offering is completely voluntary. You may contribute as much or as little as you like — or nothing at all. A boy never contributes for a girl. Each person's contribution is his own.

WHAT YOU DO
. . . when taking a trip

SOCIAL NEWS AND NOTES

Miss Elaine Carling, daughter of Mr. and Mrs. Roger Carling of 18 Oakwood Court, will spend this week end at the Phillips Exeter Academy, in Exeter, N. H., where she will be the guest of Mark Sheaffer.

Miss Erica Mendez, of Washington, D. C. is a week-end guest at the home of Mr. and Mrs. Edward L. Shane of 234 Eddystone Drive. Miss Mendez and Edward L. Shane, Jr. are classmates at Crompton Junior College.

Vernon Paoletti, of 880 Essen Avenue, will leave next Wednesday for New York City where he'll attend the International Hi-Y Conference for four days.

— You're in the news, you're on the go! And whether you're one taking a special trip to a convention, visiting the home or school of your current "big moment," or traveling with your family, it's a wonderful feeling.

Perhaps you'll travel by plane. If so, you'll probably put twenty-five cents into a slot machine at the airport and take out an air-travel insurance policy. But there's another kind of travel insurance that you're much more likely to cash in on. That's the insurance you take out when you make it a point to know *beforehand* what's expected *of* you away from home. When you're sure about travel etiquette — how to be a good guest, what to take with you, and who, when, what and where to tip — you can have a good time without worry or embarrassment.

BEFORE YOU LEAVE

Careful planning is a "must" before you start anywhere. If you're going to be staying at a hotel or motel, you'll want to write ahead for reservations so that there'll be no chance of landing in a strange place with no place to rest your weary head.

When you're going to visit friends, you exchange letters long enough before you leave so that plans are clear at both ends.

If you're going on a prep school week end with a boy friend, you probably don't have to worry about consulting train, bus, or plane schedules. If your date has been on his toes, he's told you what transportation to take, complete with times of arrival and departure.

But let's say that you've been left to make your own arrangements. In that case, you should consult your plane, train, or bus schedules well ahead of time. It may be necessary for you to make reservations. It will certainly be necessary, if you're going to be a guest, to let your hostess know the exact time and place of your arrival.

Money Matters

The amount of money you need will depend, of course, upon the kind of trip you're taking.

The boy or girl attending the school has invited you there — probably for a special week end. It's up to your host or hostess to pay for your room, meals, and admission to games and dances. You'll reach into your own pocket only to pay for: transportation — coming and going; a host or hostess gift (if you're staying with a family, rather than as a paid-for guest in a dormitory or boarding house).

A boy who visits a girl at school or college may find a few extra expenses added to these. He pays for any activity that he suggests, and which is not part of the girl's plan for the week end (an afternoon movie, post-dance snack, dinner at a restaurant instead of at the school, etc.).

He also pays for the flowers the girl wears to the dance, although some girls' schools rule "no flowers" on a girl-dates-boy week end.

As the guest of a family, you have no expenses during your stay. Your host and hostess see to it that you're fed and entertained. Even if you go out to a restaurant instead of eating at home, they foot the bill. You pay for: transportation — coming and going; a hostess gift (especially if it's your first visit); telephone calls (if you make toll calls from the family's phone).

One more word about money:

Use travelers checks.

You're tempting trouble if you carry a large amount of cash with you when you travel. One clever pickpocket, one forgetful moment when you leave your wallet behind — and your money is gone. Travelers checks, on the other hand, are numbered, so that if you lose them, they can be reported and you'll get your money back. They can be cashed only when you sign them, so they're no good to anyone else. And travelers checks are honored as money throughout the United States. They can be purchased for a nominal charge, in denominations of $10, $20, $50, $100. Generally speaking, the smaller denominations are most useful.

WHAT TO PACK — AND HOW

Inexperienced travelers usually pack twice as much as they need. The secret of efficient pack-

ing is to take only the clothes you'll need for the
things you'll be doing, and only so many as will
be necessary for the length of time you'll be
away.

Select clothes that will pack well. A sweater
would probably be a better choice than a bulky
lumber jacket if you're trying to save space in
your bag. Clothes made of nylon and other syn-
thetic materials are a boon to travelers, because
they can be washed and dried quickly.

Arrange your clothes so that the things you'll
need first are on top. (If you're traveling overnight in a Pullman, you don't want to have to
dig down under an assortment of sweaters and
underwear before you reach your pajamas.)
Fold your clothes carefully — putting tissue
paper between the folds if you want to be sure
to avoid wrinkles. Make sure that any bottles, toothpaste tubes, etc., are tightly closed.
(Note: inexpensive plastic bottles are unlikely
to break.)

Each piece of luggage should bear a tag with
your name and address clearly written on it.
Bags do occasionally get lost, and you'll have a
much better chance of finding yours again if it's
properly marked.

EN ROUTE

So here you are — your arrangements completed, your tickets in your wallet, your bags
neatly packed. It's time to go. And you hope

you'll do the right thing at the right time.

Good traveling manners are the same as good manners anywhere. The keynote is consideration of others — of your fellow-travelers, and of the people who'll serve you. Traveling by bus, plane, train, or car, you'll be careful to —

Say thank you, in the form of a tip, when tipping's expected, with a smile on other occasions. Consider the comfort of others. If you *must* have that cigarette, ask your seat companion whether he or she minds before you light up. (And needless to say, a NO SMOKING sign means just that!) Wait until you're by yourself, or with friends who love you anyway, before you begin snapping gum between your teeth or munching popcorn.

Be unobtrusive. When you're with a crowd, you may be tempted to talk and laugh loudly in public places, or even indulge in a little horseplay. Go ahead, if you like. But remember that other people will not only be annoyed — they'll write you off as a half-baked youngster who's got a lot of growing up to do. Singing and cheering may be all right on a chartered bus, where you're all one crowd — *if* you're not being so obstreperous as to disturb the driver. But it's *out* on a public bus, even if only one or two passengers are not in your group.

Be responsible. For some mysterious reason, people who take good care of their own possessions often lose all feeling of responsibility when they use public facilities. They leave rest rooms littered with paper towels, clog the toilets, leave hair combings on the sink. They walk off with hotel towels, glasses, and silverware, and don't think of it as stealing at all. They stick pieces of gum under the seats of trains, write clever remarks on washroom walls, and never put out a cigarette in an ash tray if they can find some more objectionable place for it. But of course "some people" doesn't mean *you*.

THE PEOPLE YOU MEET

One of the pleasant things about travel is that you often meet interesting people. You can enjoy these casual acquaintances and make a trip pass more quickly, *if* you keep certain "limits" in mind.

Girls

Naturally, if your mother sends you off with instructions "not to talk to anyone," you don't. But as a rule, it's perfectly all right to chat with the person in the next seat who starts a conversation. The conversation stays impersonal, of course. General topics are the rule. You'd be going beyond the bounds of your casual acquaintance if you started confessing your innermost hopes and thoughts.

If you plan to have dinner in the dining car, and your new friend asks you if you'd like to dine with him, accept — with the understanding that you pay for your meal. "Going Dutch" should make it clear that you intend to keep your relationship at the casual independent level where it belongs.

This doesn't mean that you should act as if you're intent on freezing an iceberg. Be friendly, of course; it's quite all right to talk about the country you're traveling through, discuss radio and TV, sports, hobbies, etc. Just assume from the start that your traveling companion is, like you, eager to make the time pass quickly by chatting, and that you probably won't ever see him again. That way, you can't lose — and you may win for yourself a trip that's a lot of fun.

Once in a while, you may meet someone who'll offer to drive you to your hotel or next station when your train, plane, or bus arrives at its destination. At that point, a pleasant "No, thank you" is in order. Even if it would save you a taxi fare, you don't accept a ride from anyone when you're traveling alone.

Now what about that man or woman sitting next to you whose general appearance and manner you just don't like? Or the seat companion who wants to talk when you don't feel like it? Usually, you can discourage conversation by opening a book or looking out of the window after you've made the briefest possible reply. But if he's a real pest who can't take a hint, you may have to say simply, "I'm sorry, but I don't feel like talking." If even that doesn't work, change your seat. If no extra seats are available, you may ask the conductor to move you or ask a man or boy sitting next to you whether he would mind changing.

Boys

A boy, like a girl, doesn't let casual acquaintances pay for meals or refreshments when traveling. And most of the rules of behavior that apply to girls apply equally to boys. A boy, however, will more often be interested in starting a conversation than a girl will. When he does, he should try to make sure that his overture will be welcomed. He should never begin a conversation if his companion is reading. A book or magazine is a sure sign that the other person is not interested in talking — at least at the moment. The boy should also judge from the tone of the other person's reply to his "opener" whether that person really wants to go on talking. A brief answer to a question, with no further remark, is an indication that his fellow-traveler doesn't want to get involved in a conversation. And if, after they've been talking for a while, the other person picks up a magazine or gives some other sign of having talked enough, the boy should take the hint — quickly.

OVERNIGHT TRAVEL

Planes usually arrive at their destinations fast enough so that you don't sleep on them. You'll use buses mostly for short-distance trips. Most

of your overnight travel will be on trains —
either on coach or Pullman cars.

A night on a coach is cheaper than traveling
Pullman, and many railroads now have special
night coaches. You make your reservations for
a seat on one of these coaches at least ten days
ahead of time. At a certain hour, the lights dim,
and the coach quiets down. You can rent a pil-
low from your porter, tipping him ten cents
when he brings it to you. Your seat adjusts to
a reclining level.

If you travel by Pullman, you'll probably
either have a berth, a roomette, or a bedroom.
The latter two are private rooms — with some
closet space and basin and toilet facilities — all
yours. They present few problems — all of which
the porter can solve for you.

A berth is not quite so convenient. You'll have
either a lower berth, or an upper berth which
you get into by climbing a ladder that the porter
brings you. The washroom will be at the end
of the car. There'll be just enough space inside
your berth to hang up the clothes you're going
to wear the next day.

If you have a Pullman berth, make sure that
you bring a conservative bathrobe that really
covers you. You'll be walking through the car
to and from the washroom, and meeting other
passengers on the way.

Try to be sure, before you climb into an upper,
that you won't have to come down again. It's

an imposition on the porter to ask him to bring the ladder to you too often. But if you need to get up in the night, don't hesitate to ring for the porter. It's his job to keep awake and attend to the needs of his passengers.

TIPPING

Few people think that tipping is a very desirable way of paying for services — but it's an accepted system (except on air lines where only porters at airports are tipped). The porters, waiters, taxi drivers, etc., who help you along your way are paid fairly low salaries. They count on your tips to bring their earnings up. So you tip, when it's expected of you.

The big question is: How much do you tip?

What you tip depends upon a number of things. If you go to an expensive restaurant or hotel, you'll be expected to give bigger tips than if you went to more modest places. If you're expensively dressed and traveling on a de luxe scale, you'll be expected to tip accordingly. But if you use the following guide, you won't go far wrong.

Waiter in a restaurant: 15 per cent of the bill — 20 per cent in an expensive restaurant, or if you have occupied a table for more than the amount of time necessary to eat your meal.

Taxi drivers: 10 cents for a fare of 50 cents or under; 15 cents for a fare up to 85 cents;

20 cents for a $1.00 fare; 20 per cent of
the total fare for anything over $1.00.

Hotel chambermaid: no tip if you are merely
staying the night; if staying longer, $1.00
a week.

Bellhops and redcaps: 25 cents a bag.

Doorman at a hotel: no need to tip, unless he
performs a special service for you; if he
gets you a taxi, tip at least 10 cents — 25
cents if he has had to make a special effort
to locate a taxi.

Pullman porter: 50 cents for each night in a
berth; 75¢-$1.00 for longer trips or more
expensive accomodations; add about 25 per
cent for any special attention or services
you receive. (A $1.00 tip in advance may
assure you of good service on the train, but
it is customary to tip the porter when you
arrive at your destination.)

Checking: 25 cents for checking a hat and
coat in a restaurant or hotel; 10-15 cents
for checking a hat alone.

YOU'VE ARRIVED

. . . at a Hotel

You pull up to the hotel in a cab, or arrive
by foot — if the hotel is near the station. A doorman or bellhop greets you, takes your bags, and
leads you to the registration desk (no need to
tip him for this). At the desk, you give your

name, specifying that you have a reservation, and then sign a registration card or book. This is one of the rare times when a girl signs her name with "Miss" in front of it:

Miss Constance Adler

But a boy does not use a title:

George K. Tracy

After you've registered, a hotel bellhop will take your bags and show you to your room. This is one time when you can't save money on tips by carrying your own bag. All guests are shown to their rooms by bellhops.

During the time you occupy the room, you'll be expected to observe the hotel rules. Lock your door whenever you go out, and leave the key at the desk. Don't invite any member of the opposite sex into your room. A hotel room (unless it's a suite) is a bedroom. The place to meet your date is downstairs, in the lobby. Respect the privacy and comfort of other guests — no loud conversations in your room, especially late at night; no radio or TV set tuned up to top volume.

Treat the hotel furnishings and equipment with the same care that you would at home, or when visiting a friend. And never walk off with a towel, ash tray, or anything else that belongs to a hotel. Only ignorant people think there's anything smart about that sort of thing. If you'd like that ash tray as a souvenir of your stay at the Hotel Milford, ask the manager whether he'd be willing to sell it to you. He might very well give it to you free or for a small price, but there's a big difference between asking and taking.

If you're traveling by car, you may stay at a motel, rather than a hotel. The rules for behavior at a motel are much the same as for hotels. One difference is that motels ask you to pay for your room in advance, whereas you pay a hotel bill when you check out.

. . . at a School or College

A visit to a school or college is no time to blossom forth in that "crazy" pink shirt or black velvet slacks you bought on a whim. It might be fun to appear in something off-beat at home, among people you know well, but you'll embarrass your host or hostess if you startle their school friends by appearing in something that screams for attention. Conservative good taste is important for school week ends.

Be considerate of the housemother or rooming-house keeper you may stay with. Let her know when you expect to be back in the evening — and make it a point to be back by then. She's responsible for you, and will have to answer to the college if anything goes wrong during your stay.

. . . at the Home of Friends

The minute you step into someone else's home, you begin to reveal yourself for what you really are. Ted may have seen you with a halo over your head when he met you at parties or was with you in a crowd of people. But during your visit to his home, you'll continue to rate tops with him only if you show the kind of thoughtfulness, graciousness, and sense of fitness that make the difference between an ideal house guest and one who everyone's glad to see leave.

You've been invited, let's say, because Ted wanted you to come. You may know his family only slightly or not at all. No matter. As soon as you enter the house, you're their guest, as well as Ted's. You act as interested in the rest of them as you do in Ted. You fit into the life of the family as easily and naturally as possible.

Do you help out with the housework? Yes — unless there are servants, or Ted's mother makes it perfectly clear that she'd prefer to have you keep out of the way in the kitchen. In any case, you offer assistance whenever you see something you can do, whether it's helping with the dishes or paring some potatoes. If you can get to your bed after it has aired and before someone else has made it, make it yourself.

When you do help, ask your hostess for any special directions she may want to give. Many housewives have definite ideas about how beds should be made and dishes done, and if you do things the wrong way, you won't be helping much.

Keep your room in apple-pie order. You'll be a poor advertisement of your own parents (and of yourself) if you leave pajamas or underwear strewn around in plain sight. And when you use the bathroom, make sure you don't leave it with floor wet, towels crumpled and flung to one side, toothpaste on the lavatory, or water in the soap dish.

Be prompt. If breakfast has been announced for nine o'clock, don't come straggling down at 9:15. If a drive has been planned for three, be dressed and ready to go at three. Promptness is one way of making yourself easy and pleasant to entertain.

Unless absolutely necessary, don't ask for special consideration or services. If you're on a diet and need certain foods, you should let your hostess know before you come, not after you get there. If the family drinks coffee and you prefer tea, just say "No, thank you" to the coffee — don't ask for tea. Your hostess herself may suggest an alternative to coffee, but that's her place, not yours.

Beware of borrowing. The family you're visiting may be happy to loan you a raincoat during a sudden thunderstorm, but as far as possible, you should have brought the proper clothes for everything you're likely to do. Your host or hostess has told you beforehand (or should have) what the main activities will be during your visit. You've packed accordingly.

When you come to the end of your visit, let your farewells show warmly and sincerely how much you enjoyed your stay: "Goodbye, Mrs. Carter, and thanks so much for all you've done for me. I've had such a wonderful time that I hate to leave."

Say that you wish you didn't have to leave, of course — but leave! Even if the visit has been a smashing success, and Mrs. Carter urges you to stay a day or two longer, leave at the time agreed upon before you came. The best time to leave is always before you're ready to go and before your hosts are ready to have you go! That way, a pleasant memory lingers on both sides.

WHEN YOU GET HOME

Your warm "thank you" upon parting is no substitute for the bread-and-butter letter you write as soon as you return from your visit.

In addition to writing your bread-and-butter letter, you may also wish to send a hostess gift (unless you brought one with you when you came).

You should usually send a hostess gift when
 — you have stayed more than one night on a first visit.

 — you stay frequently at the same place, and

haven't sent a gift after the last two or three
visits.

— you have stayed a week or more anywhere.

Quite often guests send a gift after the visit
because then they have had a chance to observe the needs and tastes of the hostess. The
gift may be flowers or candy (if you know what
candy the hostess likes), or anything for the
house: ash trays, special foods, such as cheese or
canned delicacies, records, linen hand towels,
etc. Personal gifts, such as wearing apparel or
jewelry, are not usually appropriate.

It's a nice extra touch to write a short note
of appreciation to anyone outside of the family
who did something for you during your visit.
Mrs. Donnelly, who gave a party in your honor,
or elderly Mr. Richter, who drove you and Ed
out in the country and took you to lunch, both
rate such a note.

If you were invited by someone besides your
hostess (her son or daughter, for example)
you'll write another letter to the person who
did the inviting. This is one occasion when a girl
does *not* wait for a boy to write first. Your
"thank you" to the boy who entertained you at
his college or prep school for a week end is as
prompt as it would be to his mother, if you'd
been at his house.

INDEX

(This index has been provided so that you'll keep this book and refer to it often. G.H.)

Who Is GAY HEAD?

● Gay Head I, who originated the "Boy dates Girl" series in *Senior Scholastic*, is Margaret Hauser, now editor of *Practical English*, another of the SCHOLASTIC MAGAZINES. She hails from High Point, N. C., where she was right in the swing of things at H.P.H.S. She played on the girls' basketball team and took part in most of the dramatic and glee club productions.

At Salem College, Winston-Salem, N. C., she wrote for the college paper and edited the yearbook. After graduation she attended the American Academy of Dramatic Arts in New York City, then returned to her home town and landed a job on the local newspaper, writing feature stories and two weekly columns. After two years on this job, she joined the SCHOLASTIC MAGAZINES staff.

Started as a monthly feature, her "Boy dates Girl" columns soon became a weekly feature by popular request and have sold out three editions in book form. She wrote "Boy dates Girl" and served as feature editor until she stepped into the editorship of *Practical English* in the fall of 1946. Since that time three others, Jean Merrill, Ruth Imler, and Nancy Scandrett, have written under the pen name of Gay Head, the "Boy dates Girl" features in *Senior Scholastic* and *Practical English*.

Both *Boy dates Girl* and *Hi There, High School!*, another book by Gay Head I, are now available through the Teen Age Book Club.

160